GHOST WRITER

GHOST WRITER

One Last Letter to America

A Viet Nam Memoir

by
Stephen Casterline

---

*Recalling the Last Dying Words
of Our War Heroes*

In order to assure privacy and protect feelings, many names have been changed and many situations have been altered. Sadly, most of this story is otherwise brutally accurate. Few have ever heard these memories because Viet Nam was not a popular war. We had no big homecoming, no cheering and, unfortunately, little thanks. There was no encouragement to talk out about our memories. After all this time, I have decided to.

Warning: Some photographs in this book are very graphic and potentially upsetting. However, it is important that readers understand the true cost of this war and a side of the story not told before.

Copyright © 2003 by Stephen Casterline.
Printed in the United States. All rights reserved.

ISBN: 1-58597-192-8

Librsary of Congress Control Number: 2003106274

A division of Squire Publishers, Inc.
4500 College Blvd.
Leawood, KS 66211
1/888/888-7696
www.leatherspublishing.com

FOREWORD

The draft dodgers and those participating in peace movements took center stage during the 1960s. They seemed to draw more attention and media coverage than our boys thousands of miles away and fighting for their lives.

The events of September 11, 2001 and the activity in Afghanistan brought back 1967 like it was yesterday.

Now it's time to tell this story — when someone might listen. A story so personal and private that it needs to be heard.

Our government is presently at war with Iraq, and I fear a war of the same magnitude or possibly worse than Viet Nam. I know about fear and pain. I know about hate and regret. And I know loss runs hand in hand with victory.

With the draft alive and well, Viet Nam became a war of teenagers. For every seasoned soldier in the region, it seems there were a dozen scared and homesick 18- and 19-year-old boys. Few of them really knew where they were or had any clue as to why they were there.

The only explanation given was that we were protecting the South Vietnamese from communism and aggression. The only obvious fact was that we were getting our butts kicked and our expendable youths were being sacrificed for a very controversial cause.

Some of us wondered if this was an attempt to create a boost for U.S. industry and at the same time reduce the number of "baby boomers" to relieve some strain from an inevitable Social Security crisis.

We underestimated our enemy and were starting a fistfight that we couldn't win or run from for so many years. And the people we came to help seemed to hate us and what we brought to their country.

I would think that for the amount of money spent, the effort and time expended and the tragic loss of lives, there might have been a wonderful alternative to this so-called "police action." Our government was afraid to categorize the activity as a war and claimed we were advising and assisting the South Viet Nam army. What a joke!

These people were largely primitive rice paddy workers, their teeth blackened from betel nuts to prevent tooth decay. A combination of tree dwellers, some living in grass huts elevated by posts above the marshland, some in caves or underground tunnels. The urbanites lived in clusters of huts, small villages very susceptible to Viet Cong raids for food and reinforcements. These villages were a perfect place for the enemy to blend in with civilians and observe our movements and become snipers when the time was right. Hundreds of thousands of our boys were sent to the slaughter.

So,

Who Was the "Ghost Writer"?

SO, WHO WAS THE GHOST WRITER?

I WAS A 19-year-old Kansas City boy, a 1964 high school graduate with one year of chiropractic college behind him and a young man with absolutely no direction in life. A couple of my best friends asked me to join the Navy with them on the buddy plan. Because the draft was eminent and Viet Nam wasn't going well, we could "join the Navy, float on a boat, and see the world." Famous last words!

The brainchild with the bright idea was Tim, our high school bad ass. The other amateur recruiter was Donnie, voted best-looking of our senior class. Then there was me, Steve, runner-up for best-looking. The margin was slight and I knew it was Donnie's Corvette that tipped the scales. If "Mr. Dimples" had to drive my car, it would have been a different race. No mention of that in the yearbook! Donnie, Tim and I were like brothers since second grade, and I knew Donnie would be crushed if he had to share the "limelight." Besides, I knew how close it was and didn't really care.

We were popular, we had the girls and rarely had more than $10 in our pockets between us. Looking back now, none of us had a lick of common sense, but we shared a closeness that was unshakable.

My high school squeeze was a debutante-style, upper-bracket, private school girl. We were an item for years, and if I wasn't out with the guys, I was with Melinda.

One evening I was invited to eat at her house, which had never happened before. Melinda's parents asked me a ton of questions as we ate and shared some information with me about their family. When we left the table, her dad asked me to join him in the den for a chat! That was the beginning of a very long evening.

After he lit a huge cigar, he began to tell me about the double wedding of Melinda's older sisters that was coming up soon. He told me that it was going to cost a bundle and he had a feeling that we would probably be getting married soon, too. Wanted to know if maybe I'd rather have a small wedding and with the money he would save he could help us out financially. Told me feeding half of Kansas City cost a lot. Said he would give me a job with his company, help with college, help us get into our first house and give us a "jump start."

Conditions of the offer were for me to convert to Catholicism and drop out of chiropractic college. He explained that chiropractic was not really socially acceptable and he wanted his daughter to have a good life.

As I sat there listening to the Beatles singing "She Loves You" on The Ed Sullivan Show in the next room where the family had disappeared to, he looked over his glasses and said, "Use your head, boy."

I had plans to marry Melinda someday, but not this soon. The way this was presented to me, I let my temper take control and said I wasn't for sale as I stormed out of the house. Melinda was no longer permitted to see me, and we broke up on her front porch a few hours later.

I knew Tim and Donnie had gone to a go-go bar called the Blue Ginger, and there was still plenty of time to drown my sorrows, so I made a beeline to join them.

As I walked in the door, a dancer was just entering a glass cage. Tom Jones' "What's New, Pussycat" was playing, and the crowd went wild. Two guys walked up to the glass cage and placed roses on the floor in front of her. I could see what everybody was excited about; she was a real heart-stopper. Her name was Maria, and she was the club's main drawing card. I doubt by the end of her set I even remembered Melinda's name. I was smitten!

After she finished a few dances, she came toward our table like a guided missile, said she had been watching me and thought I was cute. Proves my point about that best-looking deal. When the bar closed, she left with me, as all the disappointed "wanna-bees" watched me strut out in triumph.

We were a thing! I was there every night, and she was my girl. Watching her dance was a real rush, and I was falling in love again. After a couple of weeks she asked me to meet her mother one Sunday. I agreed and went to pick her up.

But there were a few surprises in store that blew my mind. To begin with, I never saw her without the make-up and a G-string before, and as the transformation began, the magic started to leak a little oil. But that wasn't the big one. When we walked in the front door of mom's house, two arm-extended children ran toward us yelling, "Mommy! Mommy!"

A six-year-old boy and a four-year-old girl. Cute, but not what I wanted to see. Maria then admitted she was 29, not 22, and had been married for several years. She assured me that I could learn to love the kids like they were my own. But I was 19, and no way was this in my plans.

The following day the three flunkateers were hanging out at the local drive-in, checking out the carhops, when we started talking about the Navy again. We decided to pay a visit to a recruiter, just to ask a few questions. It was all over in a flash. We didn't just sign up, we signed for four years. He convinced us that we could go to a valuable technical school so we could get a good job when we got out. He wasn't just a recruiter, he was some kind of a super salesman.

After some physical and written exams, we were in the Navy. Except Tim, the one who had the bright idea in the first place. He had so much to drink the night before that they found blood in his urine and turned him down.

A week later Donnie and I headed for Union Station to catch a train to San Diego, California, for boot camp. I didn't have a very big send-off crowd because of my recent breakups — parents, brother, Tim and one girl whom I had dated off and on over the years.

Donnie had a couple of girls there. He was running

back and forth in an attempt to keep them apart. Didn't work. They were talking to each other as we boarded.

Ah, yes, "Join on the buddy plan and see the world." That train ride was the last I'd see of my buddy for two years. They separated us at boot camp. After that, Donnie was assigned to a nuclear sub in Norfolk, Virginia. And I hitched a ride across town for hospital corps school.

A 14-week crash course in combat medicine — when they taught us how to draw blood on our own arm before we could do it to anyone else — was my first clue that life as I knew it had changed forever.

When corps school was completed, most of our 92 boys got orders for Viet Nam. One general's nephew and I got orders for San Diego Naval Hospital, Cardiac Care Unit. About halfway through school, an instructor, 24-year-old Lt. j.g. Rose, and I started seeing each other. She pulled some strings and kept me from going to Viet Nam. Just a few weeks later a senior nurse at the base caught us in a lip lock and reported us to the commanding officer.

Didn't take me long to have my first captain's mass. Said he would give me a choice since I didn't have many stripes to bust. I could tell Rose good-bye and be reassigned, or he would bust Rose. One of us had to fall.

The reassignment was to the hospital ship Repose in Viet Nam — considerably safer than being on land. Found out later Rose had a hand in that, too. She, I'm sure, charmed the captain like she could do so well. Beautiful girl. But she was never to pursue the relationship as long as we were both in the same service.

And so the Ghost Writer evolved.

The rest of my four-year hitch I answered to several new handles, i.e.: Doc, Medic and Swabbie. I dearly missed the name Steve.

As I boarded a huge silver prop cargo plane headed toward Viet Nam, goose bumps and a cold chill invaded my body. The cargo on this tug was row after row of wood coffins — body boxes. The oxygen dropped off the ceiling like a damp and spooky fog. I was the only passenger and had no one to talk to but myself. Just a lot of time to think about what the hell I got myself into. Maybe I should have listened to Melinda's father after all.

After the third attempt to take off, this barge finally lifted off the ground. I wasn't sure if it was the plane or the pilot having problems, but it didn't matter. The damage was done. I was scared to death.

Our first stop was in Hawaii for refueling. However, we were forced down on Wake Island first because of a typhoon. Once the storm blew over and with less fuel, it only took two attempts to be airborne. This time things were looking up!

After sleeping on a hard wooden box all night, I wasn't doing too well. Because it was October 1966, the dress code called for Navy blues when traveling. Nice heavy wool from neck to ankles. When we landed in Hawaii and stepped off the plane, I knew those blues would have to go soon. Felt like someone dumped a bucket of warm water on me.

Short refuel period and away we went; next stop, beautiful Subic Bay in the Philippines. There I was to check in with the duty officer to see if they could locate the Repose to determine if I was to continue on the same plane or stay behind. After they told me I was staying, I ran back to the airstrip to get my sea bag. It and the plane were gone. They were notified of my situation and took off. To this day I don't know if they forgot or it was a dirty trick.

They showed me a tent to stay in with a cot that looked like the Ritz Hotel to me. The base had a PX on it where I was able to buy some dungarees. After a long shower I slipped those on, and they felt like a silk suit. That shower was wonderful, cold as hell but great.

I took a nap, thinking someone would wake me up for the evening meal. When I woke up, it was about 20 minutes too late to eat. I found a guy cleaning up who sold me a peanut butter sandwich for $5 and a Coke for $2. I was starving. What a nice guy! After the sea bag incident followed by the peanut butter scam, I was about broke and suspicious of everyone.

The next morning I was the first in line at the chow hall. Those powdered eggs, chipped beef ("S.O.S.") and toast were heavenly. I even got seconds when the peanut butter salesman told his buddies about me. Then I was better rested, showered, full and in clean clothes. Returned to my tent to catch a nap when an Army guy told me I was to work KP until further notice. I did dishes and cleanup for two hours, followed by peeling potatoes for the noon meal. Never saw so many potatoes. After dinner, cleanup again.

The next morning the same pleasant Army guy took me to the latrine area. He handed me a shovel and marked off an area to dig. After I finished the hole, we pushed the outhouse over on top of it, and I was told to put the new pile of dirt into the old hole. The fragrance was indescribable in that humid 98-degree climate. That was an experience. It's amazing how much 500 men can eat and crap. Viet Nam was looking better all the time.

Day four I was jammed on another cargo plane to Da Nang. This one carried ammo, and there were some seats to sit in. You couldn't see the oxygen, and there was even another passenger to talk to. He was a lieutenant, probably 23, on his way to replace another officer who finished his hitch or was dead. His travel experience didn't hold a candle to mine, hardly any excitement at all. The difference between stripes and bars. After the third time he said, "Frankly speaking," I figured out his name was Frank.

We talked about home, our families and friends. Anything but Viet Nam. I thought I was scared, but this guy was crying and shaking the whole flight. His meltdown didn't help my thinking at all. But at least I knew I wasn't the only one who wanted his mommy.

Ah, Da Nang, upper Viet Nam! One of the safest places you could be if you were in that country. But even though the United States had occupied this area for a number of years, the base still took on occasional sniper and mortar fire. That was a bit unnerving. Weren't our perimeters protected? Why was that happening?

Once you spent a little time there, it got easier to understand. It was the problem of who's who! Seems some of the Vietnamese might work on the base in daylight, then change hats and shoot at you in the dark. One of those cute little girls might be carrying live grenades in her basket of flowers.

Everything here was in short supply. Food and water were rationed closely. They pointed me to a tent to spend the night in, but the level of hospitality was low. Everybody was going a mile a minute, choppers coming and going constantly with wounded soldiers.

This is the real thing, I thought to myself. There's an all-out shittin' war over here!

About 11:30 p.m. I woke up needing to urinate. It was pitch black out, but light from distant flares helped me find my way from the tent. I only traveled about ten steps before starting to relieve myself and heard, "Who goes there?" The flow stopped as I froze in my tracks, and there was dead silence.

I tried speaking several times, but was interrupted by a progressively louder, "Who goes there?" There's a password, I thought to myself. That's right, they told me a password. Shit! What was it? There were perimeter guards somewhere above me, maybe in a tree. I couldn't see anything. A second voice insisted, "Who goes there," from another spot.

I pissed all over myself as I ran back to the tent yelling, "Don't shoot, I forgot the password!"

Shortly after my heart stopped pounding in my chest, I heard a muffled snicker and some low conversation outside my tent. Scammed again! Hope they enjoyed that! They knew that this was a guest tent and needed a good laugh. Where the hell is this boat I'm chasing?

The following morning, before daylight, I was pushed on a chopper with a pilot, a gunner and one wounded soldier who sat beside me. Moments after taking off, I heard a series of metal tapping sounds that lasted about 20 seconds. When they stopped, a flare popped in the darkness next to our helicopter shooting small rays of light through the darkness where holes were made from sniper fire. Some of the holes were too close for comfort.

Now I began a serious meltdown and was about to see my first casualty in Viet Nam and in my life. When we set down on the flight deck, I looked over to the soldier sitting beside me, and he fell on the floor, lifeless. The triage team said no one could have helped him. He caught a round in his heart.

Seemed there was a different language used over there. The doctor who pronounced my travel partner dead looked at me and said, "Shit happens. Suck it up, sailor." Then a corpsman looked at the doctor and spouted out, "Buccu-Dinky-Dow." Later I found out that it meant "very dumb shit."

As I processed in, my travel orders were reviewed and I was told to report to the Intensive Care ward to meet my new teammates. Everyone I talked to seemed very cold and short with me. How nice, a big ship of cold steel and a big crew full of cold hearts. I was very wrong! That crew was made up of the most dedicated and caring people I would ever know in my life. And they were only short-spoken because there was no time for "nicey-nice."

ICU on the U.S.S. Repose — this is where I would

spend the next year of my life. Twenty-two bed stations, constantly rotating patients in and out, lined up in the aisles and hallways at times. Patients with eyes full of fear and tears, constantly reaching out for help.

Every day a story in itself. Every day a heartbreak of its own. And if you were rolled into Intensive Care, the saying was, "You might as well kiss your ass goodbye." It was toe-tag territory.

On top of our regular asshole and elbow pace while on duty, when we were off, we were on triage duty. That means when we heard "flight quarters" piped over the loudspeakers, we ran to the flight deck to unload patients off helicopters, stretcher them to triage and sort them for the most severe, get everyone stabilized and transport them to the appropriate treatment area. Some went to surgery, some went to the morgue, and some were sewed up and caught the next chopper back to their unit.

Flight quarters could last 20 minutes or it could last 20 hours. We always prayed it was 20 minutes because the pace was backbreaking and intense until all were cared for, distributed and at rest.

Boys came off those choppers with their guts in their helmet, with 100% body burns, with their arms and legs strapped beside their trunks in hopes they would be reattached.

The screaming, begging and crying made it hard to hear the doctors' instructions. What a nightmare! Each of those boys in their own private hell. We did all we could to help them, but it seemed it was never enough, and they were mostly kids, 18- to 21-years-old. How sad!

I got so wrapped up in the pain and the dying that keeping a grip on reality became harder by the day. I lived and breathed my patients and worked many double shifts and occasionally triple shifts. You never had to look very far for someone needing help, and our entire crew worked to the point of total exhaustion to ease the suffering.

We were constantly talking with the patients about their girlfriends, their wives and kids, the past and the future. Anything to keep their spirits strong and their will to live intact — they always had a fight on their hands to escape the ICU ward. Some of them begging us to let them go, let them die — it got pretty heavy at times and very sad.

Most of that year I pulled night duty on the ward. It was dark at night, dragging along a floor lamp from bed to bed, watching each of them to see if they were still breathing, checking their faint pulses. I prayed everyone would make it through the night. I prayed someone else would have to tag and bag them. Not because it created more work, but because each one of those faces of death stayed with you and hurt like hell. And it still hurts 37 years later.

In the military, when a superior points, you jump. Never questioning their judgment, never even thinking about it, just do it. For about the first 30 days of my tour there, I thought most of our patients were comatose or unconscious all the time. But I later learned that they were heavily sedated with morphine or codeine. We asked the doctors if they could write more prescriptions Rx, "as requested for pain." It's hard to fight back or tell someone what hurts when you are knocked out all the time.

That made me pretty unpopular with the head nurse. She wanted her ward quiet and peaceful, and if many of those patients were alert, it would increase her nurses' workload.

The doctors sided with us, and slowly these patients were waking up more, asking for food or water, wanting to sit or move the position of their beds, asking questions and fighting back harder. The activity level now was like a night-and-day difference.

Dr. McPherson was a great surgeon, and he let the skirts make a lot of the decisions for him to keep peace. Clearly more of these boys were doing better, a little more painful for them, but by their comments they preferred the pain to being out of it.

When a nurse was off duty she had a schedule, a routine of sunbathing, doing her nails or hair, with her own officer's deck to unwind on.

Don't get me wrong, nurses played a huge role in that three-ring circus and worked very hard. But compare the day and living conditions of an officer to that of an enlisted man, and it's like two different worlds.

Around March of 1967 I helped carry a stretcher patient from the flight deck with his intestines in his helmet. He was nearly cut in half. I knew he was serious, but what I didn't know was that he was about to become my personal problem. As we placed the stretcher on the examining table, one of the doctors looked at him for a moment, turned to me and said, "We could lose 10 others while we work on him. You know where everything goes, you know how to suture. Start an IV, get some blood in him, move him to the side and get busy. Sew up his bleeders, remove all the fragments and debris, clean him up the best you can, and I'll be back to check on you when I can. The OR is full, we are overloaded, and you are his only chance. You can do it."

Several hours later I put the last suture in an abdomen that looked like a patchwork quilt, started a fifth liter of blood and rolled him to ICU where I hoped someone would open him up again and make sure I did everything properly after things quieted down.

That never happened. When I returned two hours later for my shift, he was just as I left him. He looked pretty good considering what he was like earlier that day, but he was burning up with fever. The doctors told me to drop an NG tube down his nose and start an ice water lavage to his stomach. His blood count was down, and the doctors suspected an abdominal bleeder; the ice water hopefully would clot the bleeder. After about the fourth pan of ice water, the fluid began to clear, and his fever was also breaking from the cold flush. I then started him on an antibiotic and hung another unit of blood, and he was sleeping like a baby.

Later that evening I checked his NG tube again to make sure there was no more blood, and my personal problem awoke. I asked him how he felt, and he replied, "Like shit. What happened?" I explained what he had gone through and asked him his name. I knew it from his dog tag, but figured we might as well meet each other formally. He said, "I'm Dave," and told me he thought he'd died after seeing his stomach. I assured him he was doing well, and that rest was what he needed more than talking with me. With that, he closed his eyes and was out like a light. His color was good, vitals stable and temperature doing a little better.

After a well-earned rest, I reported back to the ward about 10 p.m., anxious to see how my project was doing.

The corpsman coming off duty updated me on the patients, reviewed medications and gave instructions for the night.

We sat for a while, looking over the ward, and his final comment was, "Look out there. Not one of them over 20 years old, and damn few will see 21 years."

I replied, "Bunch of shit, isn't it? What in the hell are we doing over here? Nobody stateside wants this war, and I read in the paper how they are spitting on guys when they get off the airplane after Nam. What the hell are we doing here?"

The following morning the age factor changed. We took in a 33-year-old sergeant and a couple of Army Corps of Engineers in their 30s who had all gotten caught in a napalm drop. They all had 100% body burns, and every inch of their bodies was a blistered mess. They were totally blind.

The sergeant was a big boy, and the doctors instructed us to put him on a Crutchfield bed. He was going to be difficult to turn or even touch, and the bed itself flipped over, which would make changing his dressings much easier and keep pressure points from becoming a problem because we could flip him every hour. His name was Thomas Murphy from Chicago, and he informed us that he had to live because his wife was due to deliver a baby and he was going home. He screamed constantly, more pain than drugs could overcome. By the time we finished cleaning and dressing him, he looked like a gauze-wrapped mummy.

The two engineers were dead within a few hours; neither of them ever came to. Their burns were so severe that flesh was falling off their bones. They never had a chance.

The next morning at mail call I finally got a package from home. As I read a couple of letters and rummaged through the care package from Kansas City, the mail courier called out, "Thomas Murphy." I asked him if it was for Sergeant Murphy from Chicago, and he replied it was and that his unit asked him to bring the mail to the Repose. I took it, and after throwing away nearly everything in the package because of spoilage, I carried the letter back to ICU for the Sarge.

He was asleep when I walked on the ward, but I turned his bed upright and he came to. I told him I had a letter for him. Would he like me to read it to him? He said, "Hell, yes!" As I opened it, several pictures slid out with a four-page letter.

He had a new daughter, "Maggie," and she and mom were just fine was the opening sentence. I thought he was going to jump out of the bed, he was so excited. I described every feature in the pictures and read the letter to him several times. He made me hold the pictures to his eyes to try to see, but it was useless, because he was blind.

The Sarge insisted I tuck the letter in his bandages

so someone could read it again later.

After I passed out meds and did vital signs, he asked me for pain medications. He said, "Doc, can you write a letter to my wife, please?" I pulled a stool next to him and told him I would be happy to. He told me if I let on how bad his burns were, he'd have my ass.

The letter took forever, changing words, starting all over again, had to be just right. It started out with:

Honey,

I've burned my hands so I'm letting a friend write this for me. I love you so much and thank you for our beautiful daughter. She looks just like you. I'm the luckiest man in the world to be loved by you. The doctor says when I recover I'll be coming home. I'm coming home, honey, as fast as I can.

I was reluctant to write some of the words; according to the doctors we had little chance of saving him. Trying to balance his electrolytes and prevent infection was a tall order. Staph infections ran rampant over there, and he was one big open wound. His will to live was so strong that we all hoped he could beat it.

He fought hard, and we changed bandages daily as he screamed and cursed. We selectively removed dead tissue, coated him with Betadine and poured the fluids and antibiotics in him, reading his wife's letter to him over and over, the strongest medicine we had.

He was getting weaker and weaker, and the letters were getting shorter and shorter, repeating the same words, "I'm coming home, honey."

The fifth day I think he knew he was slipping because he wanted to write a letter to just Maggie. He told her a few things about her daddy and mommy and said, "I wish I could have been there when you were born so I could give you a big kiss." He also apologized for the time he wouldn't be there in the future, "because a soldier has to go to war sometimes to protect their little girls and boys." His words got weaker and weaker, and it was like he was telling her good-bye in case he didn't make it.

He fell asleep when we finished and never came out of the sleep again. The seventh day he was gone. We lost him! The sadness came over the ward like a cold blanket as we prepped him for his long journey home. This was the toughest thing I'd ever seen. As I tucked his letter and pictures in his bandages, I thought to myself, "He never got to see his baby and she will never know him." What a waste! What an ending to a life that will touch so many others forever.

There wasn't a dry eye in the house as we wheeled him to the cooler. Two of his closest bunkmates asked if someone would help them write a letter home. I guess what happened brought a lot of emotions to the surface, and they felt a need to get in touch with a loved one.

The letter writing became infectious. Once they knew writing home didn't compromise their manliness, the requests came fast and furious. If a recovering patient was being transferred to another ward, they would educate the newer patients that we would write letters for them. And so we did! One after another, all hours of the day and night, nonstop.

Sometimes we had patients long enough to get reply letters back from the states. Hard to believe an occasional "Dear John" letter came back. Fortunately, most letters were positive and reassuring and for sure the best medicine around.

Dave never wanted to do a letter; he was bitter and felt he was going to die. Said he joined the Marines because his parents had divorced and he didn't want to live with either of them. He was in a lot of pain, and he had a problem with infection in the peritoneal area (stomach).

I would always reply that he was a pain in the ass and he was going to make it whether he wanted to or not. Told him I'd invested too much time in him to let him take the easy way out. He was staying right there with me until he was strong enough to go home because he owed me a cold beer someday.

Dave was never well enough to Medivac out or bad enough to give up on. And eventually he broke down and wrote his mom a letter.

Mom,

I should have stayed in school like you told me to. Viet Nam sounded like fun when I joined. Thought it was going to be like a long hunting and camping trip. Boy, was I wrong! If I ever get home, I'll never touch another gun as long as I live.

I'm on a hospital ship with a big hole in my stomach. The doc says I was pretty messed up, but they all think I'm going to make it. I'm scared and tired, Mom. Keep thinking this is a bad dream and next time I wake up, I'll be home in bed. But I keep waking up here over and over, and it hurts so bad.

I can taste your fried chicken now; these guys are trying to starve me to death. All I get are liquid things, soup, milk, runny pudding and lots of ice water.

When Dave started to fall asleep, I added a note myself. Told Mom he was going on a bland soft diet in the morning, and he was doing better every day. I also told her I would make him write her again soon and not to worry.

Now, more than ever, I was determined to keep him alive. Finally he started to make progress. His attitude improved, his strength was coming back and he was eating like a horse. This created a new problem. What goes in must come out, one bedpan after another. I told him if he didn't get well enough to go home soon that I was going to sew his asshole shut. Then admitted it was a good sign to see his plumbing working so well.

One blustery day we were hooked up with a cargo ship taking on supplies. Before the transfer of goods was complete, the sea swelled and a storm hit us like a hammer. Before it was over, a large swell turned the cargo ship and ran it into the side of the Repose — a big hole and a big break for our crew.

During the impact I was at the top of the stairs with a crate of apples in my hands. The crate and I went down the stairs like a rock, bouncing and flipping in the air to crash at the bottom. My back was bad, but I had some time to recover because we were dry-docked for repairs in the Philippines for ten welcomed days.

During the Subic Bay stay we had a chance to rest a little and play a little and the opportunity to transport most of our patients back to the States.

Much to my delight, Dave finally headed home. We had a little going-away party for him because his recovery had been a real miracle. He actually smiled and was pleasant as we wheeled him out the door, and after his chopper lifted off I took a deep breath and had a feeling of renewed strength.

I always thought I'd hear from him someday, but I guess he wanted to forget about the hellhole where he had nearly died.

We headed back to the war after the ship was repaired. Our normal routing was two miles out from Da Nang up the coast to Dong Ha and Chu Lai. Never out of chopper range.

While our beds were available, we took in many Vietnamese patients. Anyone needing medical assistance was welcome. We were delivering babies, doing eye surgery, heart surgery, reconstructive and plastic surgery. We even had a few POWs. Most of the Vietnamese were dark olive in complexion, averaging 5 foot nothing, but one POW was about 6'4" with a lighter complexion and different eyes. Our interpreter attempted to talk to him and threw up his hands while he commented, "Chinese." We knew that the Chinese were supplying weapons and technical advisors to the North Viet Cong, and here was the proof.

My favorite POW was a young Vietnamese soldier about 17 years old. He had head and abdominal wounds, both legs and right arm bandaged and out of commission. Every time anyone got into range, he would spit at them. As I bent down to retape his IV, the little jerk stuck a fork into my neck with his left hand. Hurt like crazy, but did little damage because he was too weak to do it properly.

We decided he was feeling good enough to travel at that point, so we dropped a dime on him and returned him to someone who wanted him more than we did, the United States Marines.

As they placed his stretcher down on the floor of the chopper, the fool hung a lunger on the gunner's cheek, probably a big mistake. He might have spit at the wrong guy.

Why was he so full of hate? Did he think our hospital bed was a torture rack? Didn't he know we were trying to help him, or didn't it matter?

Another Vietnamese patient who comes to mind was a young lady from a brothel. She caught a bullet in the forehead. She had a clean hole slightly larger than a quarter centered above the top of her nose. No way to operate. She was going to die or be a lead head for the remainder of her days. We suctioned blood and debris from the hole, bandaged it up and watched. She lay comatose for a week. One day she woke up, sat up and began to talk. Her English was fairly good as in her line of business she needed to talk to Americans. She confirmed that some Viet Cong and Americans got their appointment times crossed and a gunfight ensued.

Within a few more days she was up and around and attempting to sell her wares on the ICU ward. Our nurses decided she could go home then.

Then there was a 70-year-old heart patient. We called him George, after George Burns. Short, with Coke bottle bottom glasses. George was with us for several weeks after his heart surgery. One day when I came on duty, he was sitting up in bed eating an ice cream cone with his left hand and holding an opened *Playboy* in his right. He had a smile like he was a million-dollar winner. This old-timer was in heaven, and I'm sure he thought we were angels and he was dead. Electricity wasn't a part of his vocabulary, let alone all the gizmos and equipment on a hospital ward.

We barely changed the sheets from George's bed before it was occupied again. A 25-year-old lieutenant from Tennessee, Benny. A nice-looking, tall, slender mess. He stepped on a Bouncing Betty land mine, designed to get the job done. Small ground charge elevating the larger charge into the air where it could do upper body damage as well. Benny lost his left eye, one leg and one hand. Head and abdominal wounds were gushing blood everywhere.

We worked on him nearly five hours. He probably had a hundred small shrapnel wounds to go along with the bigger problems, but they all had to come out and be bandaged up. We nearly filled a surgical pan with metal before he was allowed to rest.

Even as torn up as he was, he kept asking about his buddies who were with him. We didn't have any information about them, but he kept calling out their names. The morphine and the hours of surgery were starting to wear him down. He was also talking about how he would tell his girl about this. We told him after he got some rest we could help him with that.

He was a tough cookie, never losing consciousness, never complaining. He was mad at the world and very aware of his condition. It looked like he was going to make it, only he didn't want to. "Let me die. Let me die," over and over.

A few days later while I was cleaning his wounds and redressing them, he said, "Steve, I need to talk to you about something."

"Sure," I said, and pulled a stool over beside his bed. He told me how he had only had six days to go when he found the "Betty." Said his girlfriend was planning their wedding in a couple of weeks and she had to know. He wanted me to write a "Dear Jane" letter for him. Didn't want her around or to see him when he got stateside.

As he wished, we began to write. I convinced him to tell her that if she still wanted him in one year he would marry her, but not now. That he loved her enough to postpone the wedding because he cared for her. He was afraid that she would pity him enough to go through with it and regret it later. He insisted I detail his injuries and tell her that he was only half a man now.

I did what he said, but added my own paragraph and introduced myself to his bride-to-be. I told her that I thought Benny was the most whole man I'd ever known. Brave, tough and my personal hero. I told her that his plumbing was still fine, and if I were gay I'd marry him in a heartbeat.

Ten days later we wheeled Benny to the communication tower where his girlfriend managed to get patched through to the ship by telephone. The signal was weak, but the love was strong. She said that she would hold off on the wedding just as he requested, but if he thought he was getting out of this wedding that easily he was wrong. And as long as he would have her she would never stop loving him.

My God, the waterworks! I thought I'd dehydrate myself from crying. This was the best medicine in the world for Benny.

One day General Walt did his monthly rounds on the ship handing out Purple Hearts. When the group got to Benny's bed, the commendation speech was interrupted. Benny told the General to go to hell and stick the ribbon up his ass.

As Walt shook his head, a tear rolled down his cheek. He was speechless and darted from sight. I guess generals weren't supposed to cry.

Benny still had a lot of healing to do and a lot of hate to vent. I was sure once his girlfriend got hold of him she would straighten him out. At least, that's what we all hoped. Sadly, most of our patients left us without us ever knowing how things turned out for them. Maybe that was for the best!

Twenty-five years later I found Benny's name on the Viet Nam Wall in Washington, D.C. His name was too unusual for it to have been anyone else. What happened? Was his chopper shot down? Did he die from infection or a sniper bullet? All I knew was that Benny died, and I sobbed uncontrollably.

As if this journey hadn't already presented enough tortuous situations, we hadn't seen anything yet.

How about hundreds of burn victims topped off with a dozen shark bite unfortunates? One after another in waves of patients for days at a time.

A jet taking off from the U.S.S. Forrestal dropped a fuel tank on the flight deck of the ship. A wave of jet fuel flooded down through the lower compartments, burning everything in its path. To escape the flames or extinguish burning flesh, people jumped off that ship from tremendous heights into the deep, dark water below.

The sharks began their feeding frenzy. The sea was red with blood, and bodies bobbed in the water helplessly. I wasn't sure if I could take much more — the horrible stench of burning flesh, the death toll rising rapidly, the endless hours of surgery and fighting back the tears so I could see what I was doing. They were dying on us, and I wanted to join them.

I was so tired after 72 straight hours, I fell on the deck outside to deep breathe and close my eyes. I'd spent every ounce of energy and emotion in my body.

As I lay there, I thought an angel was talking to me, or maybe it was God himself. A voice, soft and empathetic, told me he appreciated what we were all doing, thanked me for everything and told me to rest now. I opened an eye and looked up, expecting to find the heavenly being, only to see a young man in a wheelchair with arms and hands bandaged up. He had received burns and completed his treatment. There was no room inside for him, and I looked beyond him and saw dozens more bandaged and very glad to be alive, waiting outside in the fresh air.

I slept for a while and returned to the ward for

rounds four and five. I couldn't even remember what a good night's sleep felt like. All I knew was my Dad's favorite line kept coming through to me, "This too will pass." If there was ever a time I wanted my father to be right, it was now. It took several weeks before we got back to the normal hellish pace we were geared for.

The letter writing became overwhelming. If a burn victim had one good hand and one good eye, we had him writing for those less fortunate.

Hundreds died, hundreds were severely burned and sent back to the States, and hundreds were patched up and sent back to duty.

As I walked down the main corridor one afternoon, a young man asked me if I remembered him. I told him I was sorry, but, no, I didn't. He said he was the one who talked to me on the outer deck when I came outside to rest. I laughed and told him what had gone through my head when I was half asleep. Come to find out, he was a corpsman who had just reported to duty on the Forrestal a couple of weeks ago. He said, "Do you guys work this hard all the time?" I explained to him that would be impossible and that he and his shipmates almost did us in.

I asked him if he was hungry and wheeled him down to the chow hall. He was going back to the U.S. tomorrow and had seen a lot in a few weeks.

The ghostwriting hit a wall suddenly. We hadn't been in port for a long time, and everyone, including the ship store, was running out of paper. We used masking tape to cover old mailing addresses on the envelopes and reused them, but paper was a problem.

We found info sheets in supply boxes and used the backs of them. We even wrote letters on the backs of other letters. Anything to keep it going. It gave kids hope. It made them feel there was something to live for, that there would be a future. Letters gave them a chance to vent their hostility against a relentless enemy.

Our boys had some rugged basic training before they landed here, but the Vietnamese had a heritage and culture involving war for decades. We were playing on their court, and the net just got higher every day.

Every toe tag affected so many other lives, each casualty breaking hearts thousands of miles away. Our jobs didn't stop at the door. Our duty extended across the water as well. A dying man's final words needed to be heard. What would any of us pay for one more conversation with a loved one before they die?

As we wrote all these letters, we almost knew what they were going to say before they said it. "I'm scared." "I want to come home." "It hurts." Many saying, "I think I'm going to die." Some wanting to die.

One night about 2 a.m., I was doing rounds checking vital signs, when a voice spoke out from the darkness. I realized a moment later it was a patient who had been in a coma for days. He was a "crainy," a head wound requiring brain surgery. His name was Butch, and he had lain motionless since his arrival. He told me while he was resting he heard a woman's voice talking about him, and she said she didn't think he was going to make it. About four hours before I had heard our nurse say just that while she was going over the charts with me. Pays to be careful what you say around someone in a coma. They might know what's going on around them, but are "just resting."

I put some glycerine on his lips and gave him some ice chips to wet his mouth. Couldn't let him drink with a swelling brain, but he felt much better after that. Our conversation was brief, and he slipped in and out of consciousness.

Before the shift was over, Butch was calling out again. As we talked, he told me that he thought he was going to die. He then asked me if I would write a letter to his younger brother. My relief was due anytime, and I thought, why not? Let's give it a try. By the time I got some paper and sat down, he was out again. I whispered in his ear, "Butch, can you hear me?"

He replied, "I told you I'm resting. Are you ready to write?"

Bobby,

If you get this letter, it's because I died in Viet Nam. There is a $10,000 life insurance policy in your name. I didn't get to stay in school, and as a result it's over for me. Do not drop out of school! This money can help you. Stay in school until this shit is over in Nam. You take care of Mom!

Butch

He gave me the mailing information and told me to mail it only if he died. If he pulled through I was to destroy it. I assured him I would and he went back to sleep.

Did he fight his way out of the coma because he wanted to write his brother?

After I got some sleep and ate some lunch, I stopped by the ward to see what was going on. Butch's bed was stripped. He arrested about two hours after I left him.

I got a chance to call home from an R&R about a week later and had a long talk with my 17-year-old brother. He would have stayed in school anyway, definitely got all the brains between the two of us, but I just wanted to make sure.

When you see something like what Butch did, it really hits you how unselfish and courageous these boys were. Makes you do a little soul-searching of your own.

Within a few short hours you can get very close to someone in these situations, and you can't do enough for them. It never got easier with the numbers and the repetition. Each person with an individual face, personality and story. Each one wanting to live and wanting to say good-bye if they didn't. By now I'd lost count of the letters I'd written, and sadly had lost count of the deaths. Just too many!

A few nights later we were cruising along the DMZ a little farther from land to stay out of range from artillery fire. The loudspeaker screeched for an announcement, but much to our surprise it wasn't flight quarters this time. They were announcing a movie. A sure sign we probably wouldn't have company that night. The movie turned out to be a war documentary about Pearl Harbor. The crowd booed until the Captain explained his reasoning.

He wanted us to realize that we were lucky. Pearl

Harbor was much worse than what we had been through. Hard to imagine the small medical staff caring for all those wounded under a storm of bombs and machine gun fire. We were lucky!

While we had been dry-docked in the Philippines, three corpsmen and two doctors chipped in and bought a case of vodka. We smuggled it aboard and transferred the booze to empty IV bottles. Each bottle was marked, "Do Not Use, Cardiac Department Only," and signed by our heart surgeon. The nurses never did get wise to the stash.

After the Pearl Harbor movie, we all met on the flight deck and used up one of the bottles. It was time to unwind for an evening, and we all slept like a log that night.

Before we could find empty beds due to long-term burn victims from the Forrestal, we got hit again.

Our boys were good fighters over there. They were well-armed and ready for trouble. You wouldn't want to surprise one of them in the middle of the night. Well, it happened! One command of our boys on night recon stumbled off course and ran head-on into one of our companies dug in for the night. Someone spooked and fired a round into the darkness at a noise, and all hell broke loose. Before the firefight stopped, over 70 Americans were hit.

Many days passed again before our staff felt sunshine on their faces, and if we slept it would be a quick nap on an outer deck for fresh air. We got so tired that the hard deck felt like a down mattress.

Because of all the commotion, other patients were complaining about "holding it down," they were trying to sleep. Ammo and surgical instruments dropping into stainless steel pans, bedpans clanking and conversation did get noisy.

After about a 20-minute nap following my shift, "flight quarters" were called again. We carried several boys off with a combination of bullet wounds. They were the point men of their unit who ran into a sniper.

As I worked to get the uniform off one of the boys, he was trying to talk to me over the triage room racket. He kept asking me about the 70 we had gotten in several days ago. "You know the ones ... where it was all Americans. Where we fought each other by accident." He was curious about one of his buddies, but I didn't recognize the name. Told him "he must have been too healthy for me to meet him because he never made it to ICU." He seemed relieved until I threw in "or not healthy enough."

Then he told me that he was the one who shot the first bullet that night and nobody would talk to him. He had been scared ever since it happened and thought he was shot by someone in his unit, not a sniper like the other two. His name was Barry. He was from Ohio. Nineteen years old. His wounds were from the side, not the front like the others. One of the others looked over at him and said, "You probably turned to run, you asshole." There obviously was some tension about it. When I took him down to surgery, I asked the surgical corpsman to save his slugs after he removed them and explained why. He dropped them off later to me, said they were M-16 slugs, but reminded me that the V.C. had some of those, too.

I looked for the young man on the after-surgery ward and handed the bullet fragments to him. One of them had hit a lung, and he wouldn't be going back to his unit. He would go back to the U.S. He cried and said, "Thank God! They wanted me dead." He told me how everything came down that night and sobbed his head off. I told him, "It was a mistake. Anybody that wasn't nervous that night was either a liar or crazy." Told him somehow he had to put it behind him. Told him to go home and drink a case of beer for me.

The following week he caught a chopper and headed back to "the world," our pet name for home. I wouldn't have bet a nickel that he wouldn't put a bullet in his own head someday. How in the hell could you live with that on your back? Every time I lost a patient it bothered me bad.

Our guest list was so full all the time that they turned our sleeping compartment into a lounge for outpatients waiting for a chopper back to their units. Our bunks never went empty. Every time we wanted to get some shut-eye, we had to kick a grunt out of our bed.

Some of those boys using our bunks looked and smelled like swamp rats and hadn't bathed in weeks. They left us a little token of their appreciation — crabs! Not the Chesapeake Bay type of crab. These were little creatures that were trying to eat us alive. They were everywhere. All clothes, mattresses, sheets and pillowcases were dragged in the sea to wash away the little monsters.

Out came the razors, and not one of our corpsmen had a hair left on his body. We looked and felt like plucked chickens. Then everyone bathed with Quell shampoo to kill the stragglers. The pharmacy had plenty on hand. I guess this was anticipated. I didn't see any officers loaning out their beds. They seemed to think it was funny.

The standing joke was if you wanted to get rid of crabs, you shave half of your crotch area, set the other side on fire and then stab them with an ice pick as they run into the clearing. How cute! Seems funnier now than it did at the time.

As we look back on those days, the crabs were probably not the worst thing left on our sheets. Those wet uniforms were covered with Agent Orange, swamp water and God knows what else. We would collapse on those same sheets, wearing only a pair of boxer shorts. It was too hot down there to wear anything else. We were only allowed to change our sheets once a week. Let's see, bare skin, sweat, hot sleeping quarters, Agent Orange ... not a good combination.

Years later we find out about Agent Orange, and I wonder if any of my shipmates had the same devastating skin problems that I am having and have had ever since Viet Nam. I'm thankful they did away with leper colonies because that's where I would have ended up.

Doctors always called it psoriasis. I don't think so. I've seen an awful lot of military men with the same looking stuff as I have. If it's not an Agent Orange disorder, then it has to be related to stress. One of the two has caused it, or both!

Before any of us had so much as a 5 o'clock shadow, Mother Nature reared her ugly head again. Typhoon

Nancy! What a bitch Nancy was. They called general quarters. Everything breakable had to be tied down or taped down. All our medical equipment, our IV bottles, especially the private stock ones with the vodka in them.

We were told we had about an hour before she hit, so I made a run to the chow hall. I hadn't eaten all day and I was starving. Food looked good, chicken and dumplings and some cobbler. I set my tray on a table and went to get a glass of "bug juice," an over-sweetened Kool-Aid drink. Just before I sat down, the boat jolted, my tray flew off the table and hit the wall next to it. I grabbed a chicken leg off the floor and ran like hell down to my bunk. There we used belts, ropes, etc. to tie ourselves in our racks.

I'm glad they told us to do everything. We were about to take a 12-hour roller coaster ride like no one had ever imagined.

Forty-foot swells during the main storm front, and thirty-foot waves after it passed. The sea threw our 520-foot boat around like a toy in the bathtub. If the ship had been an inch shorter, I don't know if we would have survived it. The floors were covered with puke, and as the sea calmed down the first ones out of their bunks were slipping and sliding all over the place. The odor was really pleasant as well.

About now tensions were running high, and nobody had a very good sense of humor. Nerves were raw, and I felt like if anyone said "good morning" to me, I'd choke them.

As we settled into our beds that same evening to

try to unwind, somebody ripped a fart a couple of aisles over. Rex, a Mexican from San Diego blurted out, "White men don't stink like that." Seconds later we had a fist fight that quickly turned into a race riot.

Rex was kidding around, but it made no difference, fists were flying everywhere. Hair, teeth and eyeballs, everyone hitting someone else. I doubt most of them even knew what it was all about.

Ray-Ray, the biggest of all the blacks, and I were good friends. We teamed up and separated the two walls of anger, and everyone sort of shook it off and went back to what they were doing.

Unfortunately, in our sleeping compartment there were about 100 men. Bunks suspended by chains from the ceiling, three high, about 24" apart with a 30" aisle between them. Not an area to get any peace in, that's for sure. During the next 24 hours, many small fights broke out. A lot of threats were exchanged, and this deal just wouldn't end.

The Captain got wind of what was going on and had a boxing ring erected on the upper deck. Out came the boxing gloves, and anyone with a problem got to vent it. Turned out to be a lot of fun. Some of the biggest talkers had the weakest jaws. We were all laughing and hugging each other. Blacks, whites, Mexicans, Indians, like best friends again.

Then everyone insisted that Ray-Ray and I punch it out for a sporting event. So we agreed! We traded punches so long and talked so much shit we were both spent. I was about to throw in the towel when Ray-Ray pulled his gloves off, threw them to the floor and said,

"Screw you, man. Don't hit me no more. That shit hurts." Everyone roared, and I was glad it was over. I couldn't last much longer.

The boxing contests kept going into the next day. I was offered up to fight someone from the ship's crew, "Medics versus the Swabs." Up from the boiler room came Ben, "Big Ben"! He hit me so hard I couldn't chew anything for a week. My boxing career ended after my defeat.

The wall of intimidation came down after that, and we all lived and worked together again with one common goal: help these patients, then get back home in one piece. I doubt any of the men in the compartment ever had an issue concerning racial problems again. We couldn't have been better friends. We all had red blood and all shed some that year. No one should ever be stuck in a hot and heavy war for a full year. It's just too much. There's too much pain, too much death and plenty of fear to top it off.

As the days returned to normal, the ghostwriting resumed. One letter that stuck with me was for a patient named Bob Stoud. He wandered from his tent in the middle of the night to pee and stepped on a land mine. He got to us about 4 a.m. and was a sight. We worked on his legs for hours, trying to find a piece of this to sew to a piece of that, a vein or an artery that was salvageable, but it was no use. The doctor felt he would bleed to death if we tried to save his legs any longer. He asked for an amputation cart, ordered two more units of blood and proceeded to saw them back to 6" stumps. After placing the drains and sewing them closed, we all just looked at each other. No conversation at all. We were all sick about it. Another life ruined or definitely impaired. He told us he had only been in Nam for a few days before we sedated him. Still had starch in his uniform.

Bob was wheeled to ICU for the remainder of the night for observation and ended up staying for a long time. He threw a blood clot that moved to his heart, and we almost lost him. We poured fluids and blood thinner into him, and eventually the clot dissolved. When he started waking up a little, he complained about pain in his legs. It was phantom pain. He had no legs. He wanted to know if his wounds were bad enough to send him home. He hadn't looked under the sheets yet. I assured him that he was going back home, but didn't say anything about his legs quite yet.

Bob was around 6'1" tall when he came to us, and now he was about 3'6". As long as he was resting, I figured the news could wait until he got stronger. About 2 a.m. that night there was a loud scream and cry. It was Bob. He had reached down to scratch his leg and found nothing. Then he found the other one missing, too. We moved his bed and IV poles to the hallway outside so others couldn't hear the loud conversation we would have.

He had a girl back home who had just kissed him good-bye about eight days ago, and he didn't know what to do. Bob explained how they had dated all through high school, and she was going to save her money until he came back so she could follow him to his next duty station.

He insisted he write her a letter, immediately, to let her know what happened. I got him some paper and a pen, but his hands had enough bandages on them that he was struggling and shaking too much to hold the pen.

I told the other corpsman I would be back in a while and began to write. His voice was quivering and his mind racing, and he couldn't figure out what to say. I recommended what I'd written for so many others, a "break it to them gently" letter.

Hi, honey,

Guess what happened! I stepped on a land mine and messed my legs up. I'll be coming back in a couple of weeks, but things are going to be different for us. At least it happened quickly and I don't have to stay in this hell hole very long. I'll be home soon and we'll make some decisions about the future. I'll probably have to spend some time in the hospital when I get back, but we'll make some decisions as soon as I settle in. I'll call you!

Love, Bob

He was good with that and felt somewhat better. Still a bit panicky, but calming down. He said he couldn't imagine how she would react, and I told him that if she really loved him she'd be fine with it. "Get some sleep." I injected a mickey into his IV line and wheeled him back into the ward.

Bob wrote her nearly every day, or should I say we did. He was anxious for her reply and some reassurance that she could handle it. He kept telling her a little more each time. In the fifth letter he told her he might spend the rest of his life in a wheelchair and needed her more than ever. "Please don't stop loving me."

I suggested he hold up on that one. Give her a chance to digest what he'd already written. He agreed.

A couple of weeks later while he had been on an orthopedic ward, he received a letter from his girl and read it. He asked a corpsman if he would ask me to stop and see him when I could. The first chance I got was the next morning after my shift. It was early, and many of his roommates were still sawing logs. As I whispered to him, he handed me her letter and said, "Read it." I opened it slowly, afraid of what it would say. Bob was crying. It went like this:

Bobbo,

That was fast, how did you get hurt already? You know, I've been doing a lot of thinking, and I don't know how to say this, so I guess I'll just lay it out.

I started dating a few days after you left. I couldn't sit around for a whole year. Why should I be tied down at this age? I'm sorry you hurt your legs, but I have to think of myself here.

After I received your third letter, I felt you hurt your legs bad. But at least you still have them and you'll get better — cheer up!

If I'm not going with anyone special when you get back, maybe we can pick up what we had, but we'll have to see!

I wheeled Bob outside the deck where we sat watching the ocean. Then I said, "Bob, you didn't miss much there. She wrote that letter after your third letter to her. She would have hurt you more if she did this when she found out the rest of the bad news."

As we looked down at the water rolling around below, we looked at the sea snakes curled in the water where the ship's lights shined down. Viet Nam had hundreds of species of venomous sea snakes, and it looked like spaghetti in motion. The lights attracted insects. The insects attracted minnows, and the minnows and insects attracted the snakes, and they had a buffet feeding.

I think the reason nobody ever "hari-karied" over the side was because of those snakes and what the sharks did to the Forrestal boys. I know I had no interest in it. We did have a patient throw himself over when no one was looking, but he obviously never looked down at those lights. They found his body the next day. I heard he had lost some fingers on his hand, and I wished he would have talked to somebody about it first.

Bob headed home about a week later. We dropped him off in Da Nang to catch his flight back to civilization. He promised me he would go finish college and find a nicer, prettier girl who would really love him. He thanked me, said I was a good guy and said he would keep in touch. He sent me a postcard a month later. I sent one back, and that was the last time he wrote. I hoped he was busy doing homework. I think Mother Nature makes people forget a war for self-defense, or at least buries the nightmare for sanity reasons.

One of the most memorable letters I wrote was for Paul from Springfield, Missouri. He had just turned 22 and was very quiet all the time. Paul lost his eyes and right arm from a mortar and was doing very well considering. We kept him on ICU until we were sure his head wound only took his eyes. He had a concussion to go with it, but was very much alert. One afternoon he grabbed my arm as I gave him his meds. He said, "Steve, isn't it? Would you help me? I need to write my wife." He told me they had only been married two months before he got papers for Nam. As I put his words on paper, I thought to myself, where does he get the strength to say this? What a selfless attitude. His words were:

Shelly,

You were right as usual. I shouldn't have joined the Marines. If I'd let the Army draft me, I'd probably have stayed down south country on KP duty somewhere. And I should have really stayed in school like you wanted me to. I just had to be a hero. Well, now I'm a blind hero, and I lost my arm from a damn mortar.

I don't expect you to stay married to me. I don't even want you to stay married to me. Start a new life for yourself, you don't deserve this. I'll give you a divorce and help you get a place of your own. I love you, but if you love me you'll pack and go.

I asked him if he was sure about this, and he replied, "Might as well see what she's made of. If she goes, I'll understand, and it's for the best."

Because of the heavy casualties we were dealing

with, Paul was only on the boat for a few more days. I didn't even get a chance to talk to him again after that.

About four weeks later I got a letter addressed to "Steve, Intensive Care Ward, U.S.S. Repose, Viet Nam." Shelly wrote me a note, but Paul didn't remember my last name. I thought it was cool that it made it through.

She thanked me for getting him back to her. Said she liked him better this way, he was easier to handle and a lot less likely to run away from her again.

Those thank-you letters were few and far between, and when you got one, it made your day a lot easier.

They really seemed like nice kids, and I hoped they would make it and find happiness.

We wrote letters, some happy, most sad, one word at a time, while tears dripped down on the paper, smearing the ink. If it wasn't a tear, it was sweat. We were all on a dead run, trying to keep up with our duties and still find time for compassion and patience while those boys fumbled for words or hesitated to sob and catch their breath.

Many times we shortchanged our own families or friends of a letter because of the demands on our off-shift hours.

Occasionally we had to do a letter in bits and pieces because of interruptions or our patients slipping away on us when their pain meds kicked in. Sometimes the letter lasted longer than the wounded. Sometimes when they died before we finished, I would complete a sentence or two if I knew what they were going to say anyway. Those words needed to be heard, and the letter had to go out.

If I didn't know how to finish a letter, I would add a note to the part we had finished about how peaceful they were when they slipped away. Trying to let them know he wasn't in a lot of pain, and it was more like he just went into a deep sleep and didn't wake back up.

I would hold back mailing it for a couple of days to make sure the military informed the family of the loss. I didn't want to be the one to notify them.

Back in Kansas City, Tim told Maria my fleet mailing address. She knew I'd be back in the States at the end of November, and she was trying to rekindle our relationship. She wrote constantly, informed me she had hung up the G-string and dancing and was now modeling. Her modeling was for nude photographs, and she always included a few samples of her work to try to stoke the fire. I told her there was no way I would pursue our relationship, wished her well and ended with, "… but you can send me more of those pictures any time you want."

They kept coming, and she wouldn't take no for an answer. After a while, some of the boys on the boat were paying big bucks to buy a picture of her. She really was a looker! This eventually turned into a side business for me. Navy pay wasn't squat, and I knew I was going to need a car in a few months. The photo business was staking my loan business that was already a going concern. I would loan someone $20 until payday. They were always broke, especially if they got some liberty time. When payday rolled around, they owed me $30. Pretty good return, and I always knew where I could find them.

I never felt guilty. Unlike Maria, I was always truthful with her, and if she didn't mind the world seeing her naked, why should I?

In August 1967, our boat made a wide turn and headed south for two hours. A chopper had a special delivery, and we were trying to shorten the flight time. Tom and I carried a stretcher over to the chopper as it landed, though we didn't need to. They handed me a 30-pound package bundled in a blanket. It was a little girl with the bottom of her face blown off. She was bleeding bad, and a half-empty liter of blood was dripping full speed.

There was a crowd outside the OR waiting to see how she did. Hours later she rolled through the doors and straight down to ICU. No one knew her name, and after a while since Chin was a known name in Nam and she didn't have a chin, that's what everyone started calling her.

She was cute and only a few years old. A round hit her, taking out a front section of her chin and lower gum and teeth. She couldn't stop drooling and couldn't eat. We had to tube feed her and hydrate her with constant IVs. She was scared to death and cried if no one was holding her. Not a problem. We all fought over her anyway! She became everyone's little girl and the boat mascot. Constantly trying to entertain her and teach her some words so she could understand, we said some things other than "goo-goo"! She was so tiny, you felt like she was still an infant. She learned quickly — first words she spoke were "Buccu-Dinky-Dow." She had heard it before and it made her laugh. So she would point, make her speech and laugh her head off.

Love, hungry, thirsty and cold were her first English words. Within a few weeks, we were having full conversations with her.

After a number of reconstructive surgeries, we were slowly closing the front of her mouth. Food and drink still squirted out when she was eating, but slowly she learned how to correct that with some facial contortions. The cooks made some special meals to make it easier on her, and the way she was eating I think they were covering everything with sugar.

Slowly Chin was playing or drawing and entertaining herself and began wandering around the ward. She saw her image in a high chrome floor lamp base one day and cried after she figured out what she looked like. From that day on, one of her hands would always stay in front of her disfigurement. Thank God she didn't see herself before all those surgeries. She had come a long way. Nothing slowed her appetite. She ate like there was no tomorrow and gained weight. Her face was filling out, which also helped her appearance.

Headquarters in Da Nang thought they might have located her parents or family, so the plan was to do one more reconstructive surgery on her jaw and then turn her over to an orphanage for verification. Her appearance had changed so much in the last months, we wondered if her parents would even recognize her.

A couple of weeks later we left her standing there with a nurse as she waved with one hand and held the other in front of her face. I hoped her life would be good now because it hadn't been very good up to that point. We talked about her daily and missed her terribly.

Her vocabulary even included "ridiculous." That's about enough to someday be an interpreter. Kind of summed up the situation.

The Captain made an announcement over the squawk box. Chin's mother had been located, and she was doing fine. "All she talked about was her friends on the big boat," and she was always hungry!

The applause and voices echoed through the whole ship. What a relief! Hundreds of us would have smuggled her home in our seabag if we could have.

As she watched us walk back to the chopper, tears were rolling down her cheeks. It was so hard to leave her, but now she at least had her mommy again. I think of her often, still today. I just walked down to look at her picture for a moment.

Before we returned to the Repose, our chopper pilot got orders to pick up some wounded at the battalion aid station in Da Nang. That gave me a chance to shoot the breeze with a couple of my corps school classmates — the "Swede," John Sweden, and Tim Borden, who pulled some of the safest duty out of the bunch. They both looked ten years older than they did less than a year ago. We exchanged some stories, and again I knew that I was the "lucky one."

I had personally only seen one other of our classmates come through the Repose — Rusty, a redheaded kid from Arkansas. Rusty came into triage while I was on ward duty. They wheeled him into ICU just as I was coming off shift, and I glanced at him as I prepared to leave but didn't recognize him.

That night when I came on duty, I looked at his chart and figured out who it was. He had only been a few feet away from a booby-trap in a rice paddy. The water and weeds and rice nearly skinned him alive from the tremendous velocity when they hit him. Kind of what a sandblaster does to paint. He also caught numerous pieces of shrapnel from the device that ripped through him from one side to the other.

Rusty didn't look too good. He was kind of a skinny, wiry type. Slow-talking and bow-legged. Always had a joke and always up. I couldn't believe how quiet he was now. We had him hooked up to an automatic respirator and cardiac monitor. He probably had a lot of internal bleeding by the looks of his NG tube, and we flushed him with ice water every ten minutes. It eventually cleared! He had so much raw flesh showing we treated him much like a burn victim.

As we were changing some bandages the third day, he woke up startled and confused. Kept trying to talk, and I kept pointing to the tube in his throat. Finally I got a doctor to approve the removal of the respirator tube and took it out. He was talking a mile a minute. He was trying to figure out why I was there and where he was.

Finally he settled down and listened to me, and I explained as much as I knew as I changed the rest of his bandages.

He stayed very quiet after that, not much to say and not eating or drinking much. He seemed mad that we let this happen to him.

Evidently he had lain untreated for hours after the explosion. When you are the only corpsman in your group and there is no one to help you when you get hurt, the deck is stacked against you. He lost a lot of blood and before he got to us was nearly dead. He was extremely weak and running a fever of 104° to 105° constantly. Even with medications and ice blankets, he kept at least a 103° to 104° or higher. This went on for days.

Rusty asked me to write his mother, and I grabbed pen and paper as fast as I could. His teeth were chattering, he was so cold.

His letter was brief:

Hi,

I love you, Mom.

I got hurt a couple of days ago, and it looks like I'm not going to make it.

They have some great drugs over here, and my buddy, Steve, is with me. So I'm all right, I'm just very tired. I just had to say good-bye first. Jimmy will need a car when he turns 16, so give him my Mustang. Tell him to take care of it.

I also signed up for a payroll deduction insurance policy — I think it's 10 grand. Keep Jimmy in school.

I love you.

Meat Ball

Told me that's what his dad used to call him. He screamed for more morphine, and we got it for him. I knew he was right. It was getting close to the end. I sat holding his hand for three hours after my shift was over.

We talked off and on when he woke up, then his pulse stopped. We used the crash cart on him and brought him back twice, but the third time his pupils were fixed and dilated and the doctor called the time of death.

I was nearing the end of my tour that year and not any too soon. If someone handed me a million dollars to add a month to it, I wouldn't even consider it.

Rusty had me down now — I was just about cooked. I couldn't make that trip to the morgue too many more times.

As I said good-bye to him down in the cooler, flight quarters rang out and I was off duty. I ran to the upper decks as fast as I could. That elevator was slow as hell.

When I got to the flight deck, two stretchers were on the way to triage, and one patient remained in the chopper. He jumped out on his own, holding his abdomen. I helped him down the ramp, and we walked to triage. He was a medic, too!

He had actually patched up the two boys on the stretchers after he was wounded. All of them got hit by a land mine, but the others were much closer. The doc had about a dozen small holes in his gut, but wrapped himself up and worked on the others.

When we unwrapped him, the blood was gushing with every breath. The doctors told him he was going to surgery, and he answered, "I was hoping I wasn't going to have to do that, too. Let's go."

I took his ring, his chain from around his neck with a locket and his watch, put them all in his backpack and stored them. Before I put it away, I opened the locket and saw the picture of a girl. Thought to myself,

"Won't have to write for this kid, he's just having a laparotomy and he should be fine." Much to my surprise, they brought him to ICU after surgery. The frags had hit his liver, his spleen, several in his bowel, a couple in his stomach and one very close to his spinal cord.

He woke up a few hours later. Seemed pretty good, and he asked how the surgery went. I told him he had a few problems, one of which was a colostomy, but everything went smoothly and he should be fine.

His name was Billy Wilson, from San Diego. Nice guy, also 20, and our birthdays were only two days apart. He was doing great! We played chess when I got some quiet time and talked about corpsman stuff. He also did boot and corps school in San Diego and finished school about four months after I did. He said Rose was still instructing, and all the guys fell in love with her and she was all business. Told him, "Yeah! I fell in love with her, too, but she wouldn't give me the time of day other than class." If I'd told him the truth about Rose, he probably wouldn't have believed me, and I didn't want to run the risk of pissing her off. So far she had been like my fairy godmother, and I was probably going to live through this year.

Billy was writing his girl, Tonya, every day and doing very well. I figured he'd be leaving our ward soon for an internal medicine ward for follow-up, and day four he did.

The next afternoon, one of the guys said he had a temperature spike and some bleeding inside. They watched him overnight and it got worse, so Billy was back in surgery. They looked for a frag that they missed the first exploratory. They found it, a small, flat, sharp piece lodged in-between a fold in his liver. It was infected pretty badly, and they had to remove a good-sized piece of his liver.

Back to ICU he came, temperature soaring. We poured the antibiotics into him and got an ice blanket under him to try to correct the fever. He wasn't feeling so good.

A couple of days before he had written Tonya a letter and informed her that he was coming home soon and asked her to marry him. Said he wanted to get married on his birthday so he would never forget the date, and that was only a few months off. He showed me the letter and told me how cute she was. I confessed I had peeked in his locket and agreed with him.

His temperature kept spiking; meds and the blanket kept him going, but he was a hot one. Slowly he started having a good day here and there, but would heat up if he came off the blanket. He hated it because it was freezing him and very uncomfortable.

The doctors feared the liver was failing on him, and we couldn't cut on it again. "Keep him on ice."

Billy lay there day after day with no covering, shaking, teeth chattering, asking us to do something. His temperature was slowly getting constant around 104°, then 105°. The 17th day he had been with us, he was losing consciousness, in and out. Now fever spiking to 106° and yellow-looking. His liver had shot craps.

All we could do was sit back and pray for a miracle. God must have been fresh out of miracles because he passed on day 18. We cleaned him up, toe-tagged him, and I took him for his ride. Boy, it hurt. I would have bet all I had that he would be just fine. Those days we played chess and "shot the bull." What a sad disappointment this turned out to be.

The next day at mail call the courier shouted, "Billy Wilson." I held my hand up and grabbed it. Said Billy was on my ward.

I figured it was probably from his girl, Tonya, and it was.

I took the letter down to the morgue and unzipped his bag and opened the letter. Bill and I had been waiting for this letter, and I hoped he could hear me or his spirit was looking on. I also hoped it wasn't a "Dear John!"

The words were:

Billy,

Why didn't you ask me to marry you before you left? Big dummy. Sure I'll marry you! I figured I'd have to ask you when you got home. I've never even talked to another guy all these months. You are stuck with me, baby.

I've been saving my money so I can chase you around when you come back. I'm taking good care of your car for you like I was ordered. I drive it every weekend, wash it weekly and then cover it up again. I think you love this old Chevy more than me.

I've been visiting your parents on Sundays. We eat together, trade any letters or pictures from you and hold hands a lot. They know how much I love you.

So when do you get home? I'll marry you on your

birthday or even sooner if you want. I'm so happy, sweetie.

Love you, love you, love you, Tonya

Thank God it was the answer we were waiting for. I put the pages back in the envelope and placed it with his other personal effects in the plastic bag. Maybe his girl would think he read her words and knew her answer, and maybe he heard it. Who knows?

I zipped him closed and stood there for a moment, wondering if this would ever end.

One of our guests did get a "Dear John" that same day. He had written his girl to let her know that he was homeward bound, and when he handed it to us to mail, we handed one back to him from home.

Todd had a chest wound that closed up fine and he was recovering quickly. Great! Somebody going home standing upright. Later that evening he called me over, handed me the letter and said, "Get a load of this." I told him I had to finish meds, but I'd read it in a minute. He began to cry. A few minutes later I pulled a stool next to his bed and began to read:

Todd,

A few days after you shipped out I found out that I was pregnant. A few months ago I cheated on you with Paul while you went hunting. I'm sure it's his baby! We got married a couple of weeks ago, I just couldn't bring myself to tell you. I know how fragile you are over there, but I've got to let you know.

I love you and always will, but Paul's a good guy, and he'll make a good daddy to my child. He's been great about this whole deal and offered to marry me the moment I told him I was pregnant.

Don't hate me, I'm sorry.

Love, Kate

So much for Todd! He was as low as a snake's belly. Told me how they had gone steady for years, only had sex with her twice over a year ago and how they talked about kids and white picket fences all the time. Said, "She asked me not to go hunting that weekend. Guess I should have listened."

He only stayed with us for a few more days and shipped out. Said he was going to finish college, buy the biggest house he could find near her house and put up the highest white picket fence she'd ever seen.

And I bet he did!

I told him at least he had all his parts and he could see. "And you are one of the lucky ones."

That war broke a lot of hearts in the '60s and early '70s. Lots of high school relationships shot in the foot because of immaturity and a year-long test of sincerity. Tests of commitment when an otherwise masculine specimen of a man was reduced to part of a man or a once-normal teenager was plucked from his mother's arms and thrown into a disgusting situation that would affect his normal development mentally. Thousands of drunks and druggies would become self-destructive in the years ahead.

But like the doctor said my first day on the Repose, "Suck it up, sailor. Shit happens." I was beginning to understand why they were such popular quotes. You never get used to sadness, you simply live with it and get up the next morning and put one foot in front of the other until it's over. And "this too will pass." Thanks, Dad! That slogan held me together while in Viet Nam and a few other times in my life. But I really, really needed 1967 to pass.

As I crossed out the days on my short-timers calendar, I began to think about long-legged blondes, thick steaks and buckets of beer in that order. I wanted to hug my family and see my friends and laugh at a Three Stooges show. I wanted to be safe and feel safe and stop crying in the dark when no one was watching me. I needed my brother and my car and my dog, and I wanted to work eight-hour days instead of 15-hour ones. I was just exhausted.

Finally, about three days before my year was up, my replacement showed up. Young and tender-looking with a flush in his face, and I don't even think he shaved. He had a lot to absorb in a few short days, and as I showed him procedures and duties on the ICU ward, his eyes were as big as silver dollars. I snickered when he asked, "Do you do all this every day?" I said, "Sure do, and that's just when you are on ward duty." I explained flight quarters and triage, but decided to let him find out about mass casualties and the trips to the morgue on his own. Didn't want him to jump overboard before I got the hell out of there.

When his training was nearly complete, I took him

back to the supply room and showed him our private stash of vodka and poured him a shot. Told him this was for special occasions only, and as I fixed myself a shot I told him that "occasions don't get any more special than this."

I made him promise that he wouldn't drop the ball with these patients and told him how important the letter writing was and gave him a few examples of how it helped.

I don't even remember his name, just his face and how big his eyes were all the time.

Then I shook his hand, told him that if he worked hard and stayed busy, that one day somebody would walk up to him and say, "Hi, I guess I'm going to be your replacement."

Before I said my good-byes to all the patients and staff on the ward, I was told to report to the Captain's chamber at 1700 hours in dress whites. I wondered what this conspiracy was all about. I hadn't touched any of the starched shirts that whole year, so that couldn't be the problem. Surely the new kid didn't tell anyone about the vodka that quickly. If he did, I'd kill him; he only knew about it for three hours.

As I stood outside the Captain's door, I just couldn't figure out why I was "going on the carpet" again. While I stood in front of his desk, he signed a piece of paper, walked around the front of his desk and began to read.

Hell, it was a special unit commendation! Somebody actually noticed or cared enough to get the "old man" out of his chair. It was the nurses who asked him to do it. I'm sure he didn't know anything about the medical staff, just his "boat floaters."

I've read that commendation letter a thousand times since then, every time I need to feel better about that year. I need to remind myself that I was "the lucky one," that I was in one piece and that I had done all I could for those boys. It was okay that I was okay. I then would place the framed letter back in the dark closet where I could find it the next time I needed it. Too bad I couldn't put my mind in that closet, too, so the flashbacks would stop. The faces, the voices and nearly constant sounds of helicopter props are as vivid 36 years later as they were in 1967.

As I stepped up into the chopper for my transfer, I looked around and realized something for the first time. How did I not notice how beautiful the sea was when the water was calm, and when we flew over the beach into the treeline, how beautiful the land and the coastline were? Viet Nam was a tropical paradise with waters so colorful only God could have created it. Too bad it was a "killing field" there.

After a couple of days in the air and several plane changes, I heard the landing gear moan as we began to touch down in Seattle, Washington. When I stepped from the plane stairway, I dropped to my knees and kissed the ground. I'm sure those civilians looking at me didn't understand, but who cared? What a rush, what a feeling! My whole body went limp, and my heart was racing like crazy.

Before I could head for Kansas City, I had to take one more flight, a commuter ride from Seattle to Los Angeles. In L.A. I had a long layover waiting for a standby seat. A lady, whose son was in Nam, told me that if none were available she would give me her seat and take the next flight which would be a couple of hours later. Said she wasn't in any hurry and bet that I was anxious.

As the lady and I sat there talking, I spotted a familiar face. A K.C. girl I had dated off and on in high school was a TWA stewardess based in L.A. She talked me into staying over there for a day and spending some time with her. I thanked the lady, called my parents and told them what I was doing — and checked to see what flights were available the following day.

Barbara told me that she was engaged to a pilot, but wanted me to stay with her that night for old time's sake. We walked on the beach and talked all night. We held hands and each other for hours, both talking about how it might have been had the war not separated us when it did.

I wanted to jump her bones; I hadn't been with a girl for a year. But I respected the fact that she was getting married soon. I really cared for her over the years and especially now.

We shared one small kiss as the sun came out of the ocean. She cried for a moment and then drove me to the airport. Her final words were if he didn't show up at the altar she would transfer to National Airport in D.C. where I was going for my last two years in the Navy. The tears welled in her eyes, and our hands slowly separated.

My parents were waiting at the gate as I walked from the plane in Kansas City. As I hugged my mother,

I looked over at my dad with his hand extended. Men didn't hug much in that generation, but I pushed it away and gave him a big greasy hug. He was relieved and hugged back 'til I thought I'd pop.

There had been lots of changes the past two years. Mom and Dad sold the house I'd grown up in and moved to an apartment because they were about to move to Ohio. Dad's company had sold out from under him, and the new company had offered him a job at the corporate headquarters in Troy, Ohio. My dog, Mike, was dead; he was hit by a car, so they say. I think it was because the apartment didn't allow pets and they had him put to sleep. I gave them the benefit of the doubt though. Mike was 15 years old anyway, and he had a good life. I'd miss him; he was my buddy since I was six years old.

And my brother had started to drive a car. He wasn't 15 any more. One thing hadn't changed. They still had my old bed, and after locating my old body dent, I slept for 14 hours, bone tired! Nothing ever felt better than that sleep.

Letters

Home

March 5, '66

Dear Mom,

A couple of my friends took me out for a little ice cream for my birthday. They are in my corpschool class. That's Ken on the right. He knew I was going out on a dinner date later and thought this would be funny. I ate it all and still kept my date.

*Love,
Steve*

Dear Mom,

This is the airplane that flew me from the Philippines to Da Nang on Oct. 22, '66.

No stewardess, no drinks and no "Thank you for flying World War II Airlines."

That "tug" was built to carry cargo, not people.

Love,
Steve

The money in Viet Nam tells the story and mindset of these people. A war-ravaged land for decades.

Dear Mom,

This was my air-taxi from Da Nang to the Repose on Oct. 25, '66. It took off and left me there, and I'm not sure where "there" is. When I got off it, I said good-bye and they told me we would see each other many times.

Love,
Steve

Dear Mom,

Here is my new home for a year. It's the U.S.S. Repose AH -16. A 520-foot floating hospital. Along with the ship's crew and medical staff, we sometimes have 700 or 800 patients at a time.

Gets a little crowded, but at last I'm never lonesome. Homesick, but not lonesome.

It looks somewhat like a cruise ship, but it's all business.

*Love,
Steve*

Dear Mom,

This is my uniform while I'm in Viet Nam, "Green Scrubs." It's going to be like spending a year in my pajamas.

Someday if someone asks me what I did during the war, I'm just going to tell them "Navy Medic." It will take about an hour to tell someone all the things we have to do day-in and day-out.

I learned more my first day here than I did the whole fourteen weeks of corpschool. It's intense!

Love,
Steve

Hi, gang,

This was a picture I took through a porthole window. We can't go out on the decks until it calms down some more. This was the second day of Typhoon Nancy. What a ride that was! We still have 20' and 30' waves crashing into the side of the boat.

Bye,
Steve

Dear Mom and Dad,

Our boat had a little "fender bender." We were tied up with a cargo ship taking on supplies when a storm picked up. We tried to pull away, but a wave caught the smaller boat and turned it into us. We had to head to the Philippines for repairs.

*Love,
Steve*

Dear Mom, Dad and Doug,

When we got to Subic Bay, they drydocked us for about 10 days. Now it was out of the water and we got out of the war zone. No "flight quarters," no new patients, what a relief! They nicknamed Subic Bay "Pubic Bay." Lots of the boys contracted a venereal disease while we were there. No, not me, but I gave a lot of shots during sick bay duty. The main township was called Alongapo City; it was an entertainment strip full of junk food and bars and cold beer.

Love, Steve

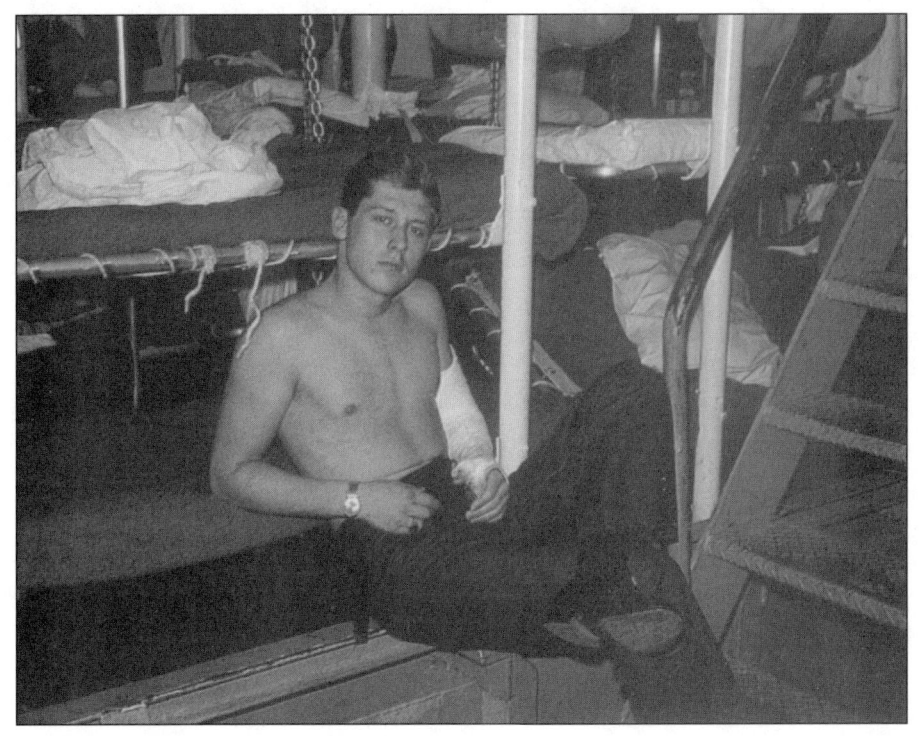

Dear Mom,

I forgot to tell you that I fell down the stairs and broke my left arm. Six weeks and I'll be good as new. It looks worse than it is and really didn't hurt that bad. Boy, does that sucker itch! Thought maybe I would be able to get off work, but that didn't happen. I've broken the cast twice lifting patients.

*I love you,
Steve*

Dear Mom,

    This is the U.S.S. Forrestal after a jet lost a fuel tank on the upper deck while taking off. The fires are out now, but all that jet fuel ran down into the lower decks, burning a lot of boys.

    We got their patients; there were 134 that died, over 300 more burned and about a dozen were shark victims. A lot of them jumped into the sea to escape the flames, and the sharks went after them.

This was a close look at hell, and none of us will soon forget it.

Love you,
Steve

Mom,

This is me writing a 2 a.m. letter, between other activities. While a patient is alert enough to dictate, you seize the moment. There might not be a second chance. If the patient falls asleep or your shift runs out, you either stay past your shift or come back later. Somehow, the letters have to get finished; they are the strongest medicine we have. When a letter comes from home, it does wonders for their recovery and spirit.

Love, Steve

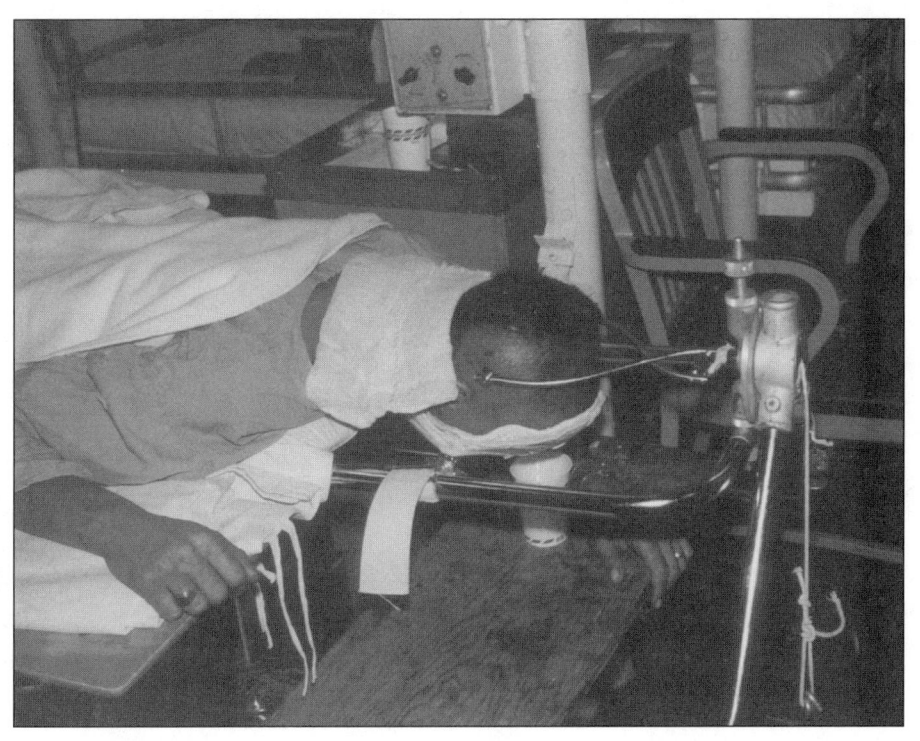

Hi, gang,

This Marine had a spinal cord injury and another round in the base of his skull. We have him on a Crutchfield bed with a special feature. The tongs in his head are connected to a rope with weights on it. It keeps tension on his spinal column to separate the vertebrae.

We tried to write a letter for him to his mother, but he doesn't stay awake long enough to finish it. Don't think he's going to make it. Bet he was a football player in school. Big boy!

Love, Steve

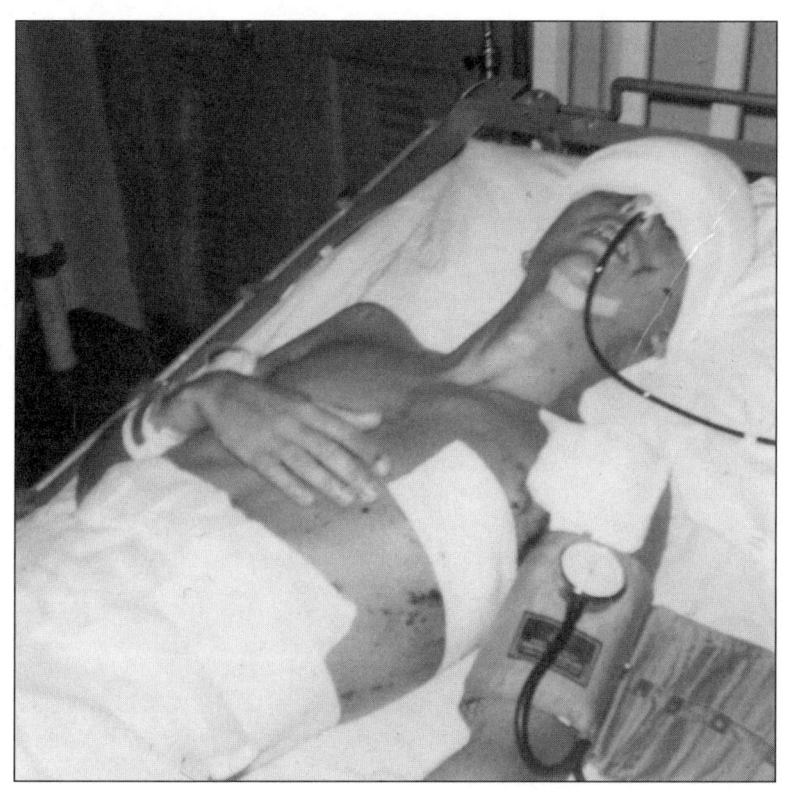

Dear Mom and Dad,

This is Benny I told you about. He was nearly finished with his hitch in Viet Nam and was going to get married soon. Those "Bouncing Betty" land mines are no fun. Benny was the one who told General Walt to stick the Purple Heart up his ass. He's a sad one!
I love you all,
Steve

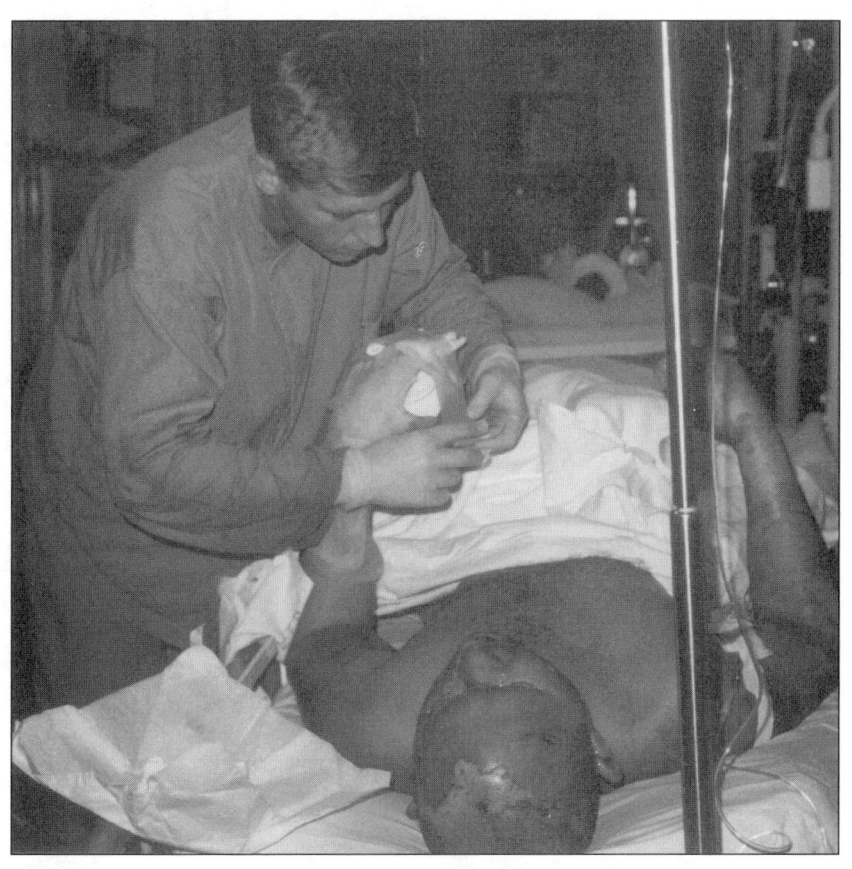

Dear Mom,

I hope some of these pictures don't upset you, but I can't really explain things any other way.

This is Sgt. Thomas Murphy I wrote you about. Severe napalm burns. He never got to see his new baby, or even her pictures because of his eyes. We lost him, he didn't make it.

Love, Steve

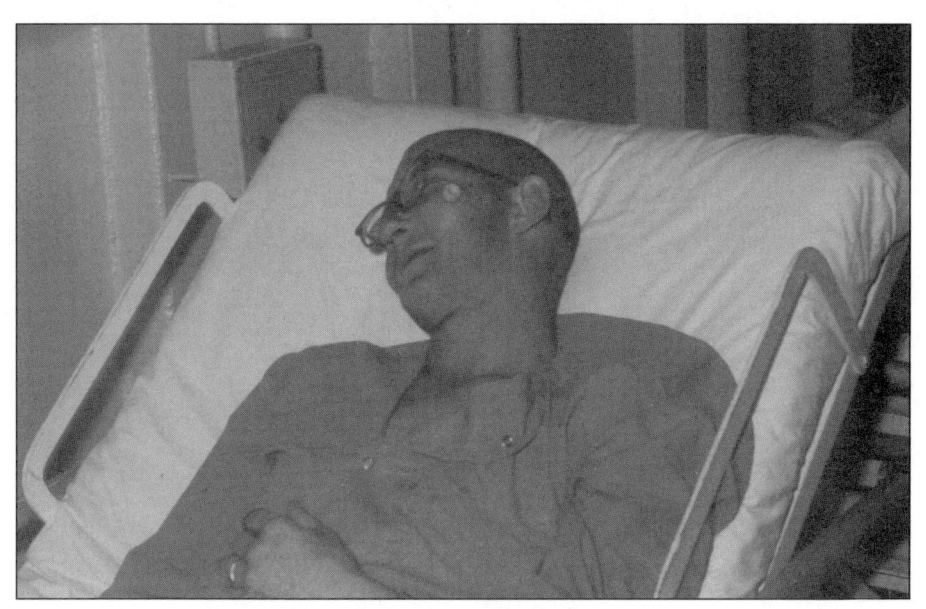

Mom and Dad,

This 33-year-old Army "lifer" is on his second tour in Nam. His name is Frank from Wisconsin. We've been talking about how good the walleye fishing is there.

He "re-upped" for a $10,000 re-enlistment bonus because he wants to pay cash for a high performance Mustang when he gets back.

He caught a bullet in his left cheek just below the eye, and it exited through his right cheek just below that eye. After many surgeries his face is healing well, but he's blind in both eyes. Anyone getting back in one piece should never tempt fate by returning to Nam.

Love, Steve

Hi, everyone,

This is what we do when we are off duty. We run to the flight deck and carry stretchers to triage and then work on them until our new guests are situated. Lots of long hours and lots of pain. Each one of these boys with his own story and in his own private hell.

I wish they would end this war, it really stinks. Never a dull moment.

Love,
Steve

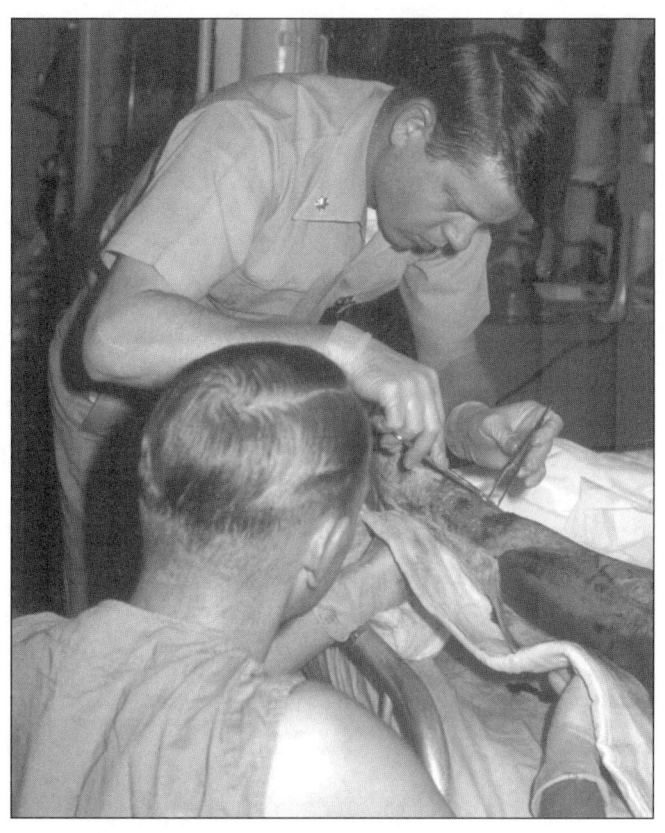

Dear Mom,

We've sure had more than our share of burn victims over here. We have to clean and redress the burns every day to allow tissue regeneration and discourage infection. The procedures are very painful and take a long time to complete.

They scream and cry a lot, and it's almost too much for them to take, or us as well.

The stench of burned flesh on the ICU ward is constant.

I love you, Steve

Hi, guys,

The nurses and doctors are always cleaner than a "Safeway chicken." White, crisp uniforms! Catch Jim, the corpsman in the P.J.'s. He looks like he's been dipped in crap and probably felt that way, too. Officers point and we do!

Shouldn't complain — with our combat duty pay the corpsmen are knocking down about 42¢ an hour. Big bucks!

Miss you, Steve

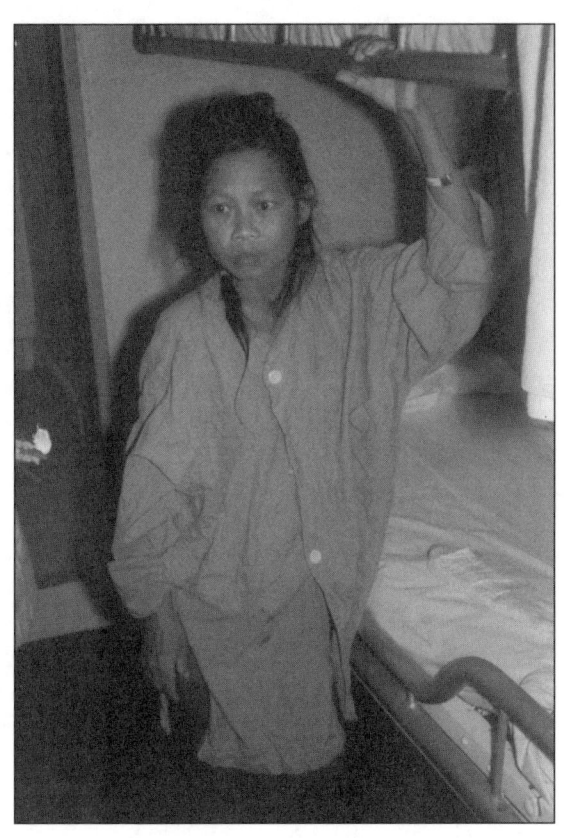

Hi, guys,

This lady lost one of her legs, and the other was torn up but salvageable. We are trading her a prosthetic leg and some physical therapy for some translating. She worked at an Embassy for years and speaks English well.

She has been a great help communicating with our patients, especially the children.

Will write soon,
Steve

Dear family,

Sometimes when the traffic is too heavy on the flight deck, the ambulatory patients are transported by boat. They might have some serious problems, but if the legs are working, "no stretcher for you."

See the low-hanging clouds; that's what I was talking about when I talked about monsoon season.

Sure wish I was home!

Love,
Steve

Hi, Mom and Dad,

These are some of the "walking wounded." Outpatients who come to us for a quick fix and then back to the front lines. Wish we could have more of them and a lot less of the critical types.

A small cut or sore on a man's foot can turn into a big problem during the monsoon season. Rains constantly, and wet boots cause a lot of infection.

Love, Steve

Dear Mom,

When we finally get a chance to crash in our bunks, we find a "No Vacancy" sign. Poor Willie had to beg to get his bed back after a long night shift. Then when you do lay down, nobody will shut up long enough to fall asleep. It's going to be a long year before it's over.

I catch a lot of catnaps on the outer decks where the air is fresh and it's quieter.

*I love you,
Steve*

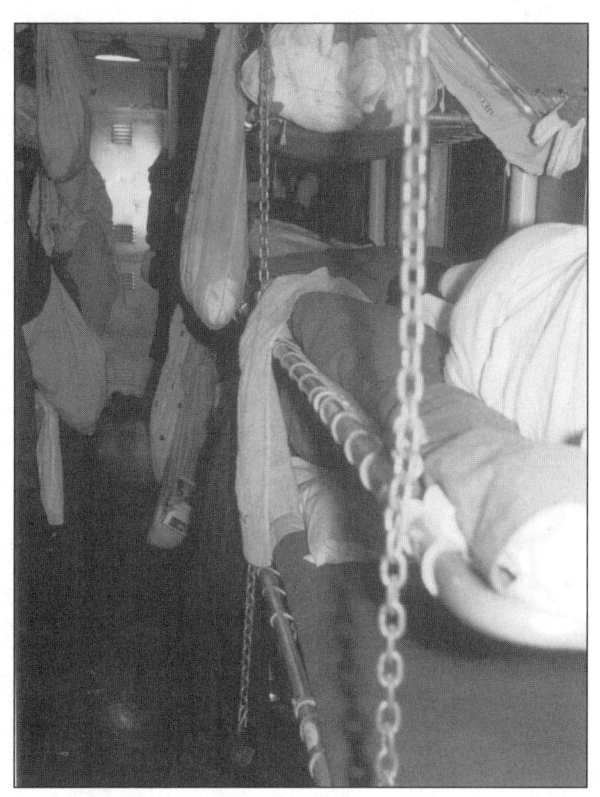

Dear Mom,

Guess I should show you the medics' sleeping quarters. Nice, isn't it? I'm sorry for complaining about sharing a bedroom with Doug for a few years. Now I share a bedroom with nearly 100 guys. In the same square footage as my old bedroom there are 12 of us stacked 3 high and 3 feet apart.

A lot of the guys borrowing our beds are fresh out of the bush. They look and smell like a bunch of drowned rats, and we only change our sheets once a week. Stinky!

Love you, Me

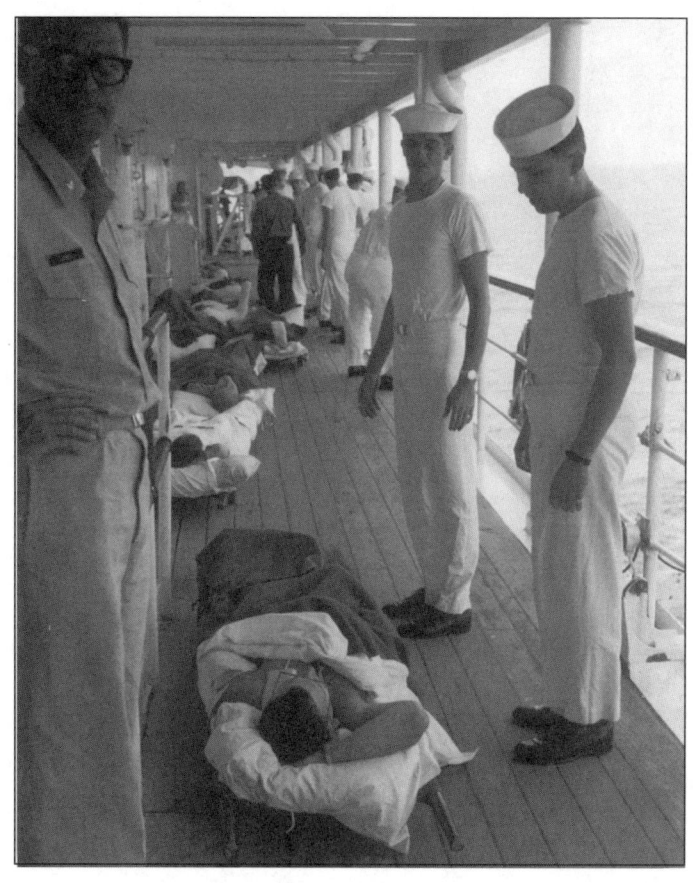

Dear Mom and Dad, Doug and Dog,

"No room at the Inn." When we get overbooked, we have to kick the better patients out to take the more serious in. Stretchers line our outer decks until we can either transport some or resituate them to different wards. It's like a revolving door, and it never stops spinning. Many times the ambulatory patients use the medics' sleeping compartment.

Love, Steve

Mom, Dad and Doug,

Here comes General Walt and his sidekicks. Time to pass out Purple Hearts and shake some hands again.

Most of the patients in intensive care were either in such bad condition they didn't really acknowledge him, or if they were alert, didn't really want much to do with him.

Like a broken record, his assistant would read the words, go through the motions, and out the door as fast as their feet could carry them. Lots of tongue-biting from all of us — a Purple Heart and a picture on the mantel were all that some parents would have to love.

Miss you all, Steve

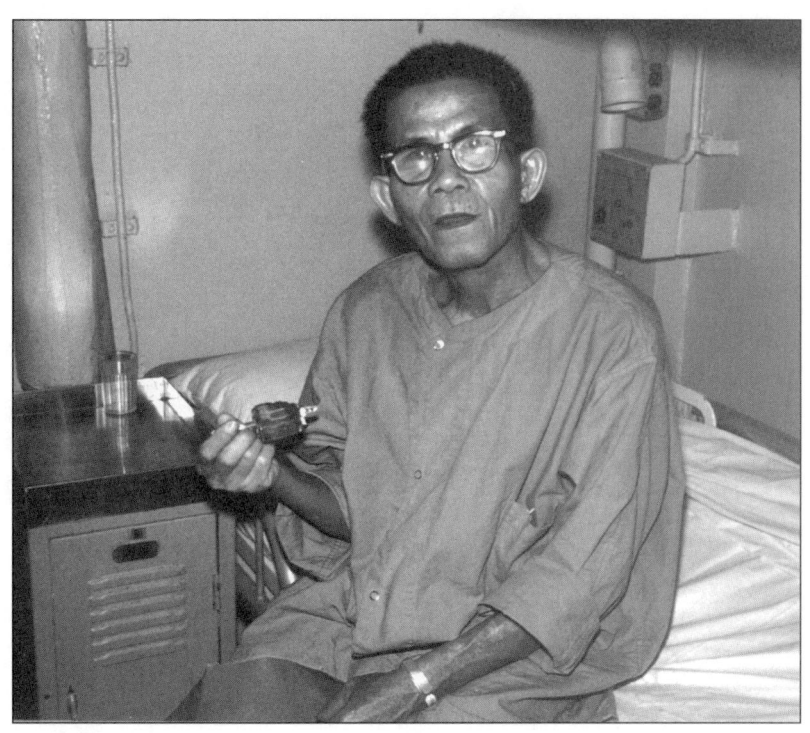

Hi there!

This is George eating our ice cream bar. He had to live 70 years before seeing a "Playboy" and tasting something like ice cream. Bet he thinks he died and is in heaven. He came to us in cardiac arrest, and after surgery he's doing great. What he tells his pals back at the village should be interesting. We're going to let him keep the "Playboy," but he may have trouble explaining the ice cream stick.

I love you,
Steve

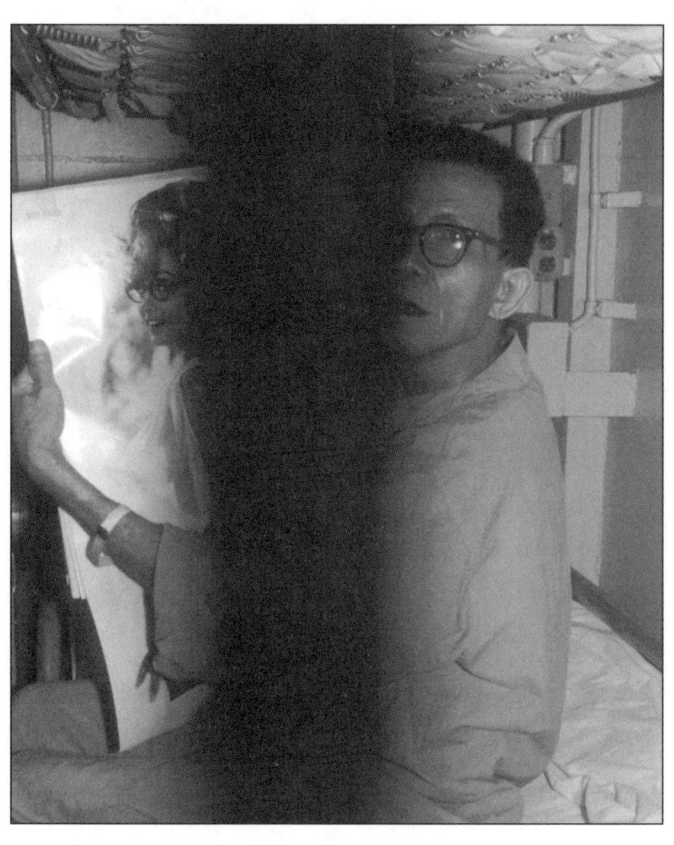

Hi, everybody,

Davis gave George his "Playboy," and we can't get it away from him. When a nurse walks by him, he looks at her and opens to the centerfold. Once in a while he gets his glasses fogged up when he gets to breathing too hard. He just had heart surgery a couple of weeks ago. Hope Miss April doesn't cause his death.

Love, Steve

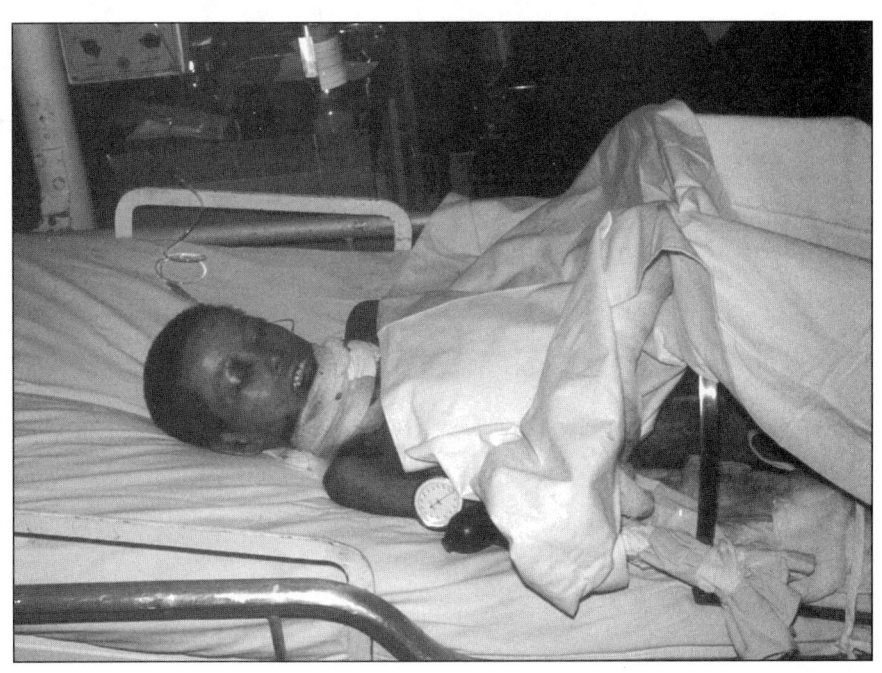

Dear Mom,

Can you believe this skinny little kid is a Viet Cong P.O.W.? He got too close to a napalm drop, too. Enemy or not, he's still just a child, and his suffering was really sad. He died, too.

Makes you wonder what kind of a life these kids have over here. As soon as they become old enough to hold a gun, they make them fight.

Now I feel bad about all the complaining I did when I was growing up. I had it pretty good, thank you!

Love, Steve

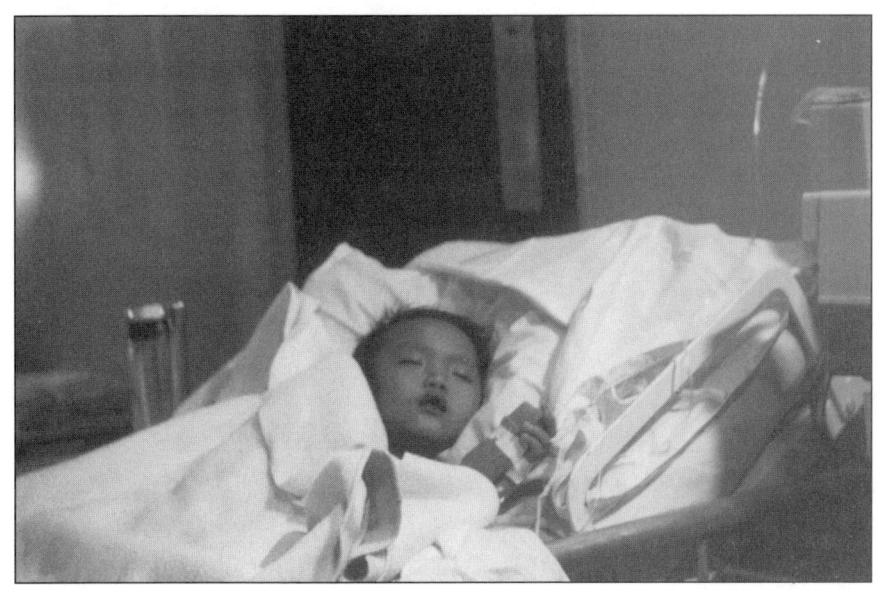

Hi, Mom,

Children and even infants aren't always immune to a stray bullet when it misses its intended target. The V.C. mix with the civilian population to hide behind them. Seems to be a popular military tactic over here.

This five-year-old little girl became a casualty statistic. She had no mommy or daddy to comfort her during her last days and moments.

These are beautiful, delicate little people trying to grow up and survive in a land of hate, death and pain.

When one perishes in front of your eyes, it's hard to handle and it makes you cry a lot.

Love, Steve

Mom,

We hear war stories every day, all day long. This infantry soldier feels that things are getting worse and thinks the Viet Cong are becoming more aggressive by the day. According to our workload, he's correct.

He will rejoin his unit tomorrow, and I wonder if we will see him again. I hope not, at least not on ICU.

I love you,
Steve

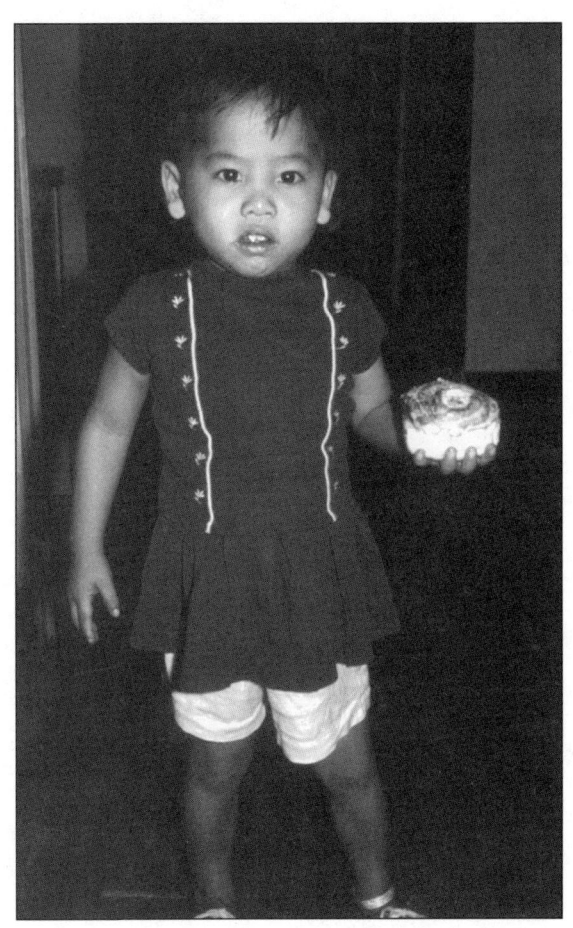

Mom,

Is she cute or what? This roll in her hand will last her for days. Her eyes are always full of fear, but she's starting to come to us to be held. There were several shrapnel wounds on her back that probably would have killed her if the Repose hadn't been handy. As soon as they recover, they go back to hell again.

Love, Steve

Hi, Mom,

Look at these children, they are so cute. Wide eyes and wondering what this place is and how we got this village to float on the ocean. Must seem like they are on a spaceship and we are aliens. They live in villages with no electricity, and ice cream is a complete mystery. If you try to hug them, their little bodies stiffen and shake. Once they get to trust us, they constantly hold out their arms to be held. How many can I bring home with me?

Love you,
Steve

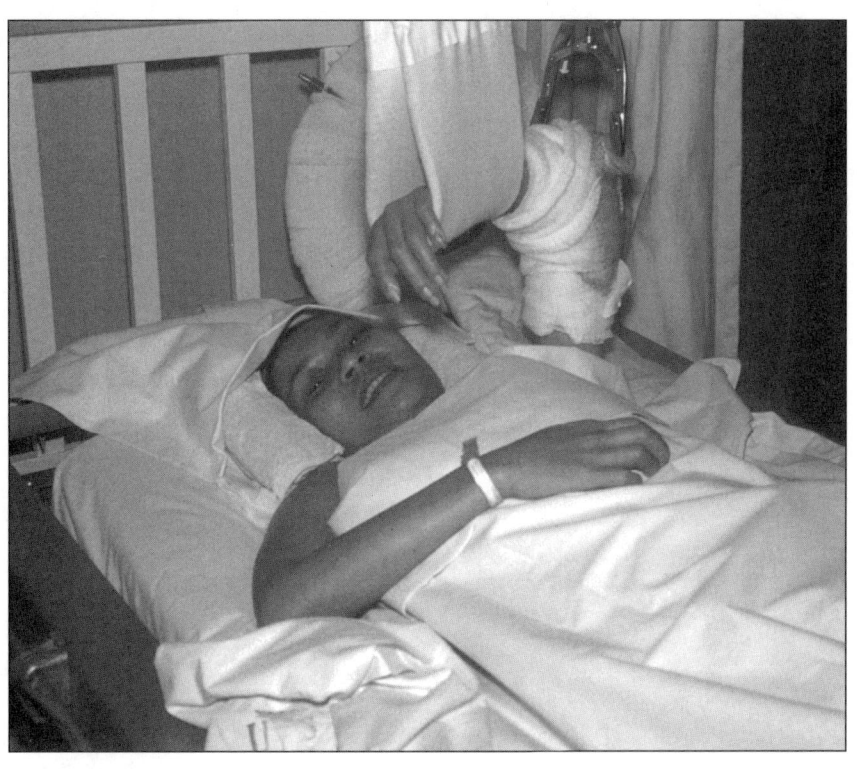

Hi, Mom,

This is a 26-year-old mother of two. A single round went through her body, severing her spinal cord at the fifth thoracic vertebrae, and still had enough velocity to shatter bone in her arm. She still doesn't know that she will never walk again. They want to get her stable before hitting her with that news. She calls me "Stebe" instead of Steve, and because I have a cast on my left arm, too, we are pals. Nice lady! Sad, too!

                                        Love you, Steve

Hi, guys,

When we can see land getting close and a supply ship hanging around, we start watching for gunships and hold our breaths. This usually means we are about to hear "flight quarters." We got closer to the beach because the boys were starting a fight again, and a long day was inevitable.

Around mid-February '67 our boat spent more of its time up north. The DMZ had lots of "hot spots." In Chu Lai, Dong Ha and Phu Bai, Operations Prairie II, III and IV were bringing in lots of casualties, and on hill 881 we lost 160 Marines and had over 700 wounded in just a few months time. They started operation Kingfisher that by October cost us 340 Americans and over 3,000 wounded. Gettin' busy!

Love, Steve

Hi, Mom,

One night a row of lights came near our boat. Faint at first, and as it drew closer, we could make out a red cross on the side of a long white boat. It was the U.S.S. Sanctuary reporting for duty. We welcomed the help; it had been a long year, and our crew was just about used up, as well as our boat. Not long after I return to the States, the Repose will start her long journey home. Not as pretty and clean as she once had been and licking her wounds. But that ship was heaven to thousands of boys desperate for help, and saved many Vietnamese as well.

Love,
Steve

Hi, everyone,

This picture shows Rusty bending down in front of me in boot camp. I remember he said, "Let somebody good-lookin' up here." Always a clown, always had a joke! Watching him lay there in ICU so quiet and weak is pretty sad. Wish I could help him. I sure wish I could come home now.

I love you all,
Steve

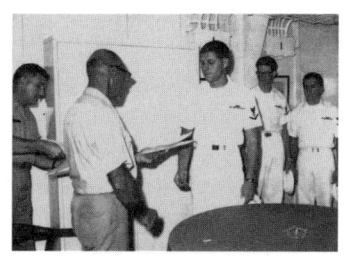

**NAVAL HOSPITAL
USS REPOSE (AH16)**
FLEET POST OFFICE
SAN FRANCISCO 96601

01:HAM:jgk
1650
11 OCT 1967

From: Commanding Officer, Naval Hospital, USS REPOSE (AH-16), FPO San Francisco 96601
To: HM3 Stephen J. CASTERLINE, USN, 999 36 16, (0000/0000)

Subj: Letter of Commendation

1. On the occasion of your transfer from this command, it is with great pleasure that I commend you for your outstanding performance of duty during the period 25 October 1966 to the present as set forth below:

> "During your tour of duty, you have been assigned to the Intensive Care Unit in this hospital. Your performance of duty has been of the highest caliber. You have demonstrated a level of skill and judgment in your nursing care of seriously and critically sick and wounded patients far superior to that normally expected. You have, with competence and zeal, worked long hours during regular schedules and during additional periods in the care of mass casualties. By your unswerving loyalty and dedication you have contributed greatly to the accomplishment of the mission of the REPOSE while in support of United States and Free World military forces in the I Corps Tactical Zone, Republic of Vietnam. Your performance has been in keeping with the high tradition of the United States Navy."

2. A copy of this letter will be made a part of your official service record.

HERBERT A. MARKOWITZ

Back to America

BACK TO AMERICA

MOM KNEW I would cover a lot of territory in my eight days of leave, so she made a big pot of vegetable soup. She knew it was one of my favorites, and that way I could warm up a bowl any time of the night or day when I got hungry. That was a good plan.

One afternoon Mom asked me to go for a walk with her down by a creek. I could tell something was wrong the way she hemmed and hawed and beat around the bush. Finally she told me that that summer she had an operation for cancer. That it was in several areas, and there was a chance it would return. She didn't tell me while I was in Nam because she didn't want me to worry about her. We held hands and walked back home quietly.

Those eight days went like a flash. I had eaten, drunk and kissed everything in sight. It was time to get on another airplane and turn to another page in my life.

Because Viet Nam wasn't fashionable, it was never the topic of my conversations. I really needed to forget about it and shake off those memories, but it's hard to do when you have to spend two more years in service, this time at Bethesda Naval Hospital in Maryland, just outside of D.C.

Hallways and parks full of wheelchairs and canes, blind people and disfigurement. Amputatees and men crying in the psych wards. They were the leftovers from a hell that lasted too long, and it was questionable if it ever should have started.

Our military would pull out of Viet Nam a few years later, tails tucked and bottom line defeated. That outcome was a hard pill to swallow for all these boys carrying their wounds and memories for what? Why did they do this to all of us? I've heard it took 10,000 rounds per Viet Cong killed. We could have won that war and turned Viet Nam into a parking lot, but humanitarian scrutiny and political ratings were controlling the maneuvers.

We would find our boys tied to a tree with their privates stuffed in their mouths. We were being killed by women and children and were supposed to abide by "rules of engagement." But who the hell was a civilian and who was the enemy?

There were generations of underground tunnels and booby-traps giving our enemy an everyday element of surprise. Snipers in trees everywhere, cheap shots from an invisible foe.

I think my new plush duty assignment was an admission of guilt. They probably figured another two years in a hands-on hospital environment and they would have to scrape me off the sidewalk. I'd had enough! National Navy Toxicology Unit behind the hospital would be where I worked for two years.

When I checked in, they explained that we would be running tests on animals to determine the toxic effects of poisons, gasses and fuels during a prolonged exposure period. After rats, monkeys, dogs and guinea pigs were exposed to various levels and types of elements, they would be monitored for changing blood levels, skin lesions and motor skills. We would eventually necropsy (autopsy) them to see what also happened to their organs, weigh them as a whole and in parts. Then we would do the same to a healthy animal, never exposed, to see the difference.

Really sad, torturing the little creatures, especially the dogs and monkeys, but I guess it was important to determine if things like Agent Orange, jet fuels, etc. could really kill people.

For the first few weeks I would hang around the hospital wards in the evening, looking for someone without eyes or hands needing some help with a letter. It's hard to break old habits, and I felt the need was still ever present, be it in Viet Nam or the East Coast.

One evening while in the chow hall, I looked across the room and spotted the "Swede" from Idaho, the big boy whom we used to tease about eating too many of those potatoes. He looked a little better than he had in Da Nang a few months ago, but still was about 40 pounds lighter than he was in corps school a year ago. His face was drawn, with bags under his eyes, and he was wearing a patient robe. He stood up, shook my hand and pulled up his pajama leg to show me his prosthetic leg. A mortar got him only a few days after we saw each other.

I pushed his wheelchair out to the park, and we had a smoke and talked into the night. Said he had to be in his bed by 8:30 or his nurse would think he went AWOL. He had a few more days of rehab to finish, then he was heading home, discharged and glad of it. I saw the Swede a couple more times, and then he was gone like so many others, but not in a body bag.

About two weeks later I found another old classmate, Dick, from Pensacola, Florida. He was on a burn unit without his eyes. He told his parents he was injured via a phone call, but didn't say exactly how bad his eyes and burns were. He didn't want to rattle them, and he knew they were in no financial condition to come up to see him.

I talked him into 'fessing-up after a few visits, and spent many evenings pulling the words out of his mouth in order to complete a letter:

Mom and Dad,

My eyes are worse than I told you, and my burns are a bit more extensive than I let on. I didn't want you to worry. I can see lights and blurred images, but am sightless for all practical purposes. I might improve and I have some, but the doctors say it's not going to get much better.

Now the burns are bad, but doing well. I'm going to look like shit, but I won't have a lot of problems with it. Hell! I can't see myself anyway, so just tell me how good I look and I'll believe you. Don't be running up here. I'm okay and I'll be home in a few weeks.

Love you, Dick

Dick wasn't okay at all. Sat around listening to his radio all day, chain-smoking, and didn't have much to say unless you pulled it out of him or he needed batteries for his tune box. His mother came Johnny-on-the-spot once she got the news. The base pastors found her a room to stay in where they were remodeling a wing of the hospital. She took two weeks' vacation from work and stayed with him until they discharged him.

I took them out to dinner at a seafood restaurant their last night and spoke positively about him going home. He wasn't buying into it much; we all knew he didn't have much to look forward to.

Dick wrote me a few times. Hard to read; he was all over the paper, but each one got a little better.

Dick was the last effort I made to help anyone. I needed to let it go, stay out of that hospital and get on with life. It was someone else's turn. Besides, the last two times I was over at the burn unit, another corpsman was writing a letter for a patient, and I knew the ball was being carried.

Okay, if I was going to get on with my life, I needed some wheels. I had saved up enough to buy a two-year-old '66 Mustang. But I needed insurance before I could go anywhere. Because I was male, under 25, military, and not living at home, I was high-risk. Didn't budget for this, but I was due for another stripe and pay raise. That would cover my quarterly payment.

I felt good about the written exam I needed to pass for my promotion, but after the test my commanding officer requested my presence in his office.

He asked me how bad I wanted that stripe. I said, "What did I do now, sir?" He said, "Nothing, and you aced your test! But because you have two full years on your hitch, I would have to send you back to Viet Nam as a combat medicine instructor. This conversation never happened, but somehow we misplaced your test, and you can take another one if you want to. You have one hour." He handed me another set of questions.

It's strange how poorly I did on that second test, I couldn't remember much at all. Only got a couple of correct scores on the whole test. I got lucky again! The C.O. was a nice guy. He could have kept his mouth shut and let me pass.

Only problem I had now was car insurance. I took a job as a bartender at the base enlisted men's club and killed two birds with one stone. I was going to be there anyway, and I might as well get paid and get my drinks free. They didn't care, just don't get drunk while on shift.

So I was covering my car insurance and gas, but still didn't have any pocket change to speak of. The Navy paid me $127.50 every two weeks, and my bartender job paid $100 per week before taxes. Tips on base wouldn't buy you a pack of smokes each week. So I was clearing about $155 per week and working about 72 hours a week.

Then I figured I'd been working about a hundred hours in Viet Nam and it didn't kill me, so I took a third job. Two hours in the morning, five days a week, drawing blood and reading lab results at a nearby civilian hospital. I was pulling down $3.50 an hour there which, after taxes, netted me a clean $185 a week for all three jobs. And only working 82 hours for it. It was a piece of cake.

That piece of cake started getting pretty stale after a couple of months; what did this do for getting on with my life? One Friday night, about an hour before my shift was over, somebody ordered a Bud. Not looking up, I put it on the bar and told him that's 30 cents. He put it up and said, "Thanks, Fish Lips." Only one person in the world called me that. It was Donnie! He found out I was working there and had driven up from Norfolk, Virginia, for the weekend.

I asked my boss if I could get off early, and he said, "No, you lock up." I tried to explain how important it was that I take off, and he still said no, so I threw him my key and quit.

We had a great weekend — so much to catch up on and talk about. It had been such a long time. The visit was the best thing in the world for me. I hadn't had any fun in so long I wasn't sure how to do it. Donnie headed back for Norfolk on Sunday afternoon, and I drew blood at Suburban Hospital at 5 a.m. Monday morning. Back to the grind! My boss at the bar wouldn't hire me back, so I had nowhere to go Monday night.

A couple of my barracks mates asked me to go into D.C. to hit a bar they had been going to lately, so I tagged along. As we sat at a table making a pyramid out of empty beer cans, a couple of locals got in a fight, knocking our beers all over us. Smitty and I each grabbed a guy, took them to the front door and threw them outside on the sidewalk. Joe took $3 out of one guy's pocket to replace our beers, and we went back in.

The owner came to our table with a pitcher of beer and thanked us as he wiped the table off. He asked if either of us wanted a job. Smitty and Joe were pretty well off and didn't need the money, but I asked more about it! Told him I had been a bartender for a couple of months, "What's the pay?"

He said he didn't need a bartender but did need a bouncer. I said, "Okay, what's the pay?" He said $4 an hour. Six nights a week from 7 p.m. to 1 a.m. I thought, let's see, six times six is 36, times $4 is $144 per week. That was more than I was making at my other two jobs put together, and I wouldn't have to get up at 4:15 a.m. any more.

I asked him, "When do I start?" He said, "See those two guys stealing the urinal out of the men's room?" "Yes," I replied. He said, "You can start now. Stop those assholes!" I did, hooked his toilet back up, and he said, "Make that $4.50 an hour." I was in heaven! Eight hours on my Navy job, six as a bouncer equals 14. My God, I had ten hours a day that I didn't have to work, part of Saturday and all day Sunday. What a deal!

That was an interesting job. It was really fun if I didn't have to get in a fight, and if I tore up a shirt or anything, the owner would always pay me extra. One Friday night I was at the club before my shift, waiting for my paycheck. I was sitting with two of my friends, Jim and John, when a 5'11" blonde, tall, well-endowed American girl, with legs to make you whimper, walked by us. The other guys were gasping for air, and I replied, "Ah, she's too tall." She was a knockout, but I was only 6'1", and with her heels she was as tall as I was.

Her name was "Charlie." Little did I know, but we would be married two-and-a-half months later! We talked at the club that night; I had a date with one of her friends the next night, and we ended up at the same party. Before the party was over, I ended up with Charlie, and we dated from then on. We were having a hell of a time saying good-bye to each other every night and figured the only way we were going to get any sleep was to get married and we did.

My friends on base took up a collection and gave us a little mad money for our wedding. After we finished the ceremony at the base chapel, we jumped into the car and headed for Ocean City for a two-day, all-expenses-paid, beach-front motel room at the Stowaway Motel. We both had to be back to work Monday morning and couldn't get any time off.

After stopping for a nice steak dinner, we checked into Room 203 of the Stowaway. It was a no-frills room with a black-and-white TV that barely worked. But we were happy. Charlie made a dash to the bathroom, promising to "be right back." After I watched a full half-hour TV program, drank half the bottle of champagne and put on one of her silk nightgowns to humor myself, she ran from the bathroom, diving under the covers like a bullet. (We've been married 34 years, and it's still hard to catch her naked.) It was February 7, 1969, and too cold to spend much time on the beach, but there was plenty to do in our room anyway.

We revisited that same room, 203, many years later for an anniversary weekend, still very much in love and still best friends.

Since Charlie was a dental assistant making the big bucks, $211 every two weeks, and I got an off-base allowance for housing, we were making a clear $800 a month. Enough to get a little one-bedroom apartment, and I was even able to quit my second job. I only had to work 40 hours a week all of a sudden. What was this? I felt like a human being for a change. With all this free time I actually had a social life, and Charlie and I had a lot of good times together.

One evening Charlie was going to meet me at the enlisted men's club for a sandwich after work. I had been there with a bunch of my friends for about an hour. By the time she arrived, all four of my friends were shaved bald by my clippers we used on our experimental animals. They were all broke, and I told them I'd pay $5 if I could shave their heads. They all agreed and looked like a bunch of white cue balls above the neck. The evening ended up being so much fun we ended up hanging around for a couple of extra hours to enjoy the baldness.

A little while after Charlie got there, the bartender walked over to our table and set a beer in front of me and said it was from the tall guy at the bar. He had his back to me, but I could see he was a big guy with a full beard. I couldn't figure out who it was, so I walked up and tapped him on the shoulder. He spun around, hugged me and said, "You son of a bitch, how are you?" I still didn't know who he was, but after looking in his eyes for a moment I recognized him without doubt. It was Dave! My project from Viet Nam. He looked great, about 30 pounds heavier and upright. I had never seen him in a standing position before and had no idea he was that tall. He pulled up his shirt and showed me his stomach and said, "I hope you aren't going to be a seamstress when they let you out."

We had a good laugh and talked for a long time. I took him back to the table and showed his belly off to everyone. He quietly asked me why I didn't let him die, but thanked me for it anyway. I replied, so he could buy me that beer he owed me when he got back, and it worked, didn't it?

I asked him where he was stationed and he replied, "U.S.S. Mom's House. I've been discharged several months now." Told me that he was at Bethesda for two reasons: to find me and to see if anyone around the hospital needed some help with their letter writing for a few days.

We ate lunch a couple of his three days and spent an evening together before he left. That visit probably was one of the best things in the world for me at that time. We hugged one more time, and that was the last I ever saw or heard from Dave. His thanks meant so much to me and seeing him laugh and walk and be alive was exhilarating.

After our first anniversary, Charlie and I were told she was going to have a baby, and eight months later she gave me a beautiful son. We had picked out several names for a boy or a girl, but the moment I laid eyes on the little guy I insisted he be Steve, Jr. What a doll! He was the second best thing that had ever happened to me in my life.

As Stevie grew up, we were like the Three Musketeers. He was just "one of the guys," going to parties and pretty much everywhere we went. We really didn't have any family around to help us with him and didn't trust babysitters.

So we figured he might grow up a little different, but he was always safe with Mommy and Daddy, and he grew up great. He's funny, quick-witted, smart as a whip, loving and totally uninhibited. Steve ended up being our only child, and what a good one he was.

The best thing that ever happened to me was his mommy. Strong resemblance to Elke Sommer, the movie star. Charlie was beautiful, statuesque, a staunch German mix with enough of a stubborn streak that she was determined that she could housebreak me, and has put up with me now for 34 years.

I nicknamed her the "Sarge" after we got married, because that sweet girl I dated learned how to give orders immediately after the wedding. When Junior was 19, he ran into a little gal named Joyce. They made a cute couple! Steve was 6'4", 210 pounds, and she was petite, about 5'5".

They have been married 11 years now and have given us the three most beautiful grandchildren anyone could ever dream of: Jordan, a nine-year-old grandson; Rylee, a four-year-old granddaughter, and the first girl on my side in five generations; and a brand-new grandson, Nicholas, six weeks old.

We are so lucky Stevie ended up with Joyce. She's been more like a daughter than a daughter-in-law and has allowed us to be such a big part of their lives. We are Grammy and Grampy and have a ball with all of them. Now we are the Seven Musketeers, and they never have lived more than a few moments away from us.

In 1999 I developed congestive heart failure at age 53. Now I'm 57 and pretty much a bed bug. I'm weak, tired and stuck in Viet Nam. It's hard to control my thoughts as my mind wanders in several directions at the same time. Catch myself talking to myself at times and hoping that no one notices when others are around. I can't imagine what life might have been like if I grew up without a war clouding my mind.

I've visited the Viet Nam Wall in Washington, D.C. a couple of times. As I walk the wall locating so many names that crossed my path while in the service, I've had many one-sided conversations and cried my guts out, tears that sometimes were held back for a number of reasons over the years. Getting from one end of the wall to the other is the longest walk I've ever taken.

When we started to leave, I couldn't help but stop and watch the guards on the wall. So straight and tall, so proud, so young. Boys with everything to live for and so much to offer. I prayed they would never see a war.

The print "Reflections" hangs on the same wall as my picture of little Chin. When alone, I'll stop before it and have more one-sided conversations. Their hands extended to mine, I can't help but speak with them on occasion.

I've spoken to pictures of my father in the past, asking him to save me a seat in the fishing boat, and as I speak to my fallen comrades, I ask them to save me a seat at the card game.

Why did I live? Why was I "the lucky one"? Was I supposed to put these memories down on paper at a time when someone might care or listen? Does our nation understand that there was a draft in the 1960s and 1970s that dragged our boys out of their element and sent them into hell?

The demonstrators who accused all of us of being "baby killers." The attitude that we had a choice in the matter. Do you all understand yet? Our boys were murdered, and those who lived were scarred physically and mentally with not only no thanks or respect, but spit on and cursed.

Was it ignorance that made those protesters pick on the soldiers rather than our government? Or was their display due to cowardice and fear for themselves or loved ones?

I said I'd never write any more letters to comfort a wounded soldier. Well, I'm writing one more. It's this book, and this time I'm writing for myself.

All I know is that I'm tired. I'm running out of positive thoughts and the resistance to not give up.

Thank you for listening to the ramblings of a confused and tired mind. And in the future, if you know or meet a Viet Nam vet, thank him and shake his hand. These are people who definitely "gave at the office."

I'm watching my tears smudge the ink again as I try to nail these memories down on paper once and for all, trying to evict the unwelcome intruders that have filled my mind with so much pain and sadness for 37 years now. They have been persistent and tireless and "my personal problem."

I dedicate this book to the men and women who served in the Viet Nam war, and hope when someone comes back from the next war you thank them and appreciate the sacrifice of those who died protecting the freedoms that have blessed so many. Freedom that is taken for granted until someone has to pay for it.

Letters to America

Dear America,

"Charlie" and I were married in the Navy Chapel in Bethesda, Maryland, on February 7, 1969.

The Captain and my boss, Jim, both told her that if I was a little late to work on Monday morning they would probably not notice. Then the Captain told her that the way she looked today, he wouldn't be shocked if I ended up AWOL. Then he winked at me and said, "Just kidding."

Her proper name, Charlene, has rarely been used. She was a born-and-raised Washington, D.C. girl and could light up a room like nobody I've ever known. She was everything I needed, and after dating only two-and-a-half months we traded rings, and it has lasted over 34 years now.

Steve

Dear America,

This is my beautiful wife and son in 1978 in our first new house! Steve Jr. was six, and my best friend, Charlie, was 28 and gorgeous. I was 32 and the owner of a very successful home improvement business.

Should have been the perfect life, but something was wrong. Seemed like I was always sad, drinking too much and having trouble sleeping.

Every time things went well for us, I would pull stunts that would have cost most men their marriage. It's like I couldn't allow myself to be too happy or too prosperous.

My thoughts of Viet Nam were constant; ceiling fans would trap my eyes and the fan blades would suddenly become helicopter props. War movies were out of the question! A familiar face, voice or situation would turn into a patient reaching out for help or calling me. Sometimes I'd find myself crying for no reason or have a fit of rage when I shouldn't

About ten years ago I learned about Post Traumatic Stress, and slowly over the last few years I've started to understand the years of confusion.

I came back in one piece, but we all left something over there. If they issued Purple Hearts for broken hearts, I'd have a chest full of them.

Steve

Dear America,

Donnie and I were coerced into singing at our 20-year high school reunion. I had to portray Willie Nelson and Donnie was Julio Iglesias, while singing "All the Girls I've Loved." I needed more hair and a beard. I've got the beard now, and our 40-year reunion is in two years. Maybe we can do it again.

We've been friends for nearly 50 years now, and I guess he's a little better-looking at this age. It's just those damn dimples; without them, he's nothing! As close as we are, I've never discussed Viet Nam with him.

Steve

Dear America,

My perfect grandson, Jordan, when he was five years old. He is being raised with all the love and security, the warmth and comfort that any child should need.

The thought of him being subjected to a war, the thought of his swingset and his playhouse turning into soldiers and death in his backyard is unthinkable.

His agenda might include video games and soccer practice at 5:30, then Chuck E. Cheese's afterward. Those Viet Nam children concerned only with hunger, survival and fear are a constant memory to deal with.

I again thank those who fought and those who gave their lives to assure Jordan's freedom and his perfect life.

Steve

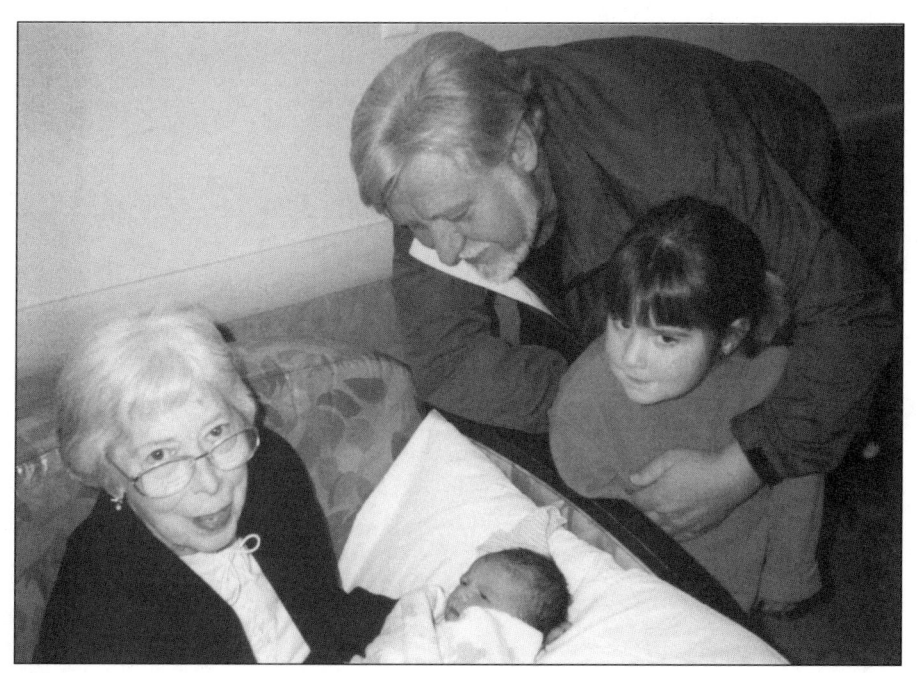

Dear America,

Mom is nearly 80 and still going strong. She had a recent bout with cancer again, but is now doing fine. I lost my dad a couple of years ago.

My beautiful granddaughter, Rylee, somehow always ends up in my lap or under my arm. She's a "snuggle bug."

And our newest grandson, Nicholas, was born two months ago, and he's another "keeper." I couldn't be prouder.

Steve

Dear America,

My wife, son and daughter-in-law and grandchildren are the glue that holds me together.

God, I hope none of them ever has to live in a war zone like Nam.

This book took me nearly four years to complete. It just hurt too much to think back and recall the mental pictures. I pray for peace. Will you join me?

Steve

Dear America,

One of my biggest inspirations for finishing this book is LiAnna. She's my next-door neighbor here in Kansas City. I've watched her grow from three months old to five years old. Her mother, Shelly Doyle, brought her back from Viet Nam when she was just an infant. I had no idea that they were going to adopt a Vietnamese child until I saw her in her new front yard. Her eyes captured mine instantly, and I snatched her away from her mother's arms without even asking. Seeing her was overwhelming. She's adorable, and her face has triggered many memories over the years.

When Shelly learned that I was going to finish a book about Viet Nam, she showed great interest and has spent many long hours helping me type my rough drafts and being a sounding board for me. Her knowledge of Viet Nam is vast, and her opinion has been valuable.

Steve

Dear America,

I introduced my son to some old friends on the Viet Nam Wall. Later we talked for hours as I sobbed and he listened.

I finally let myself break down, and he was the first person to hear me out. He hugged me, held me and thanked me for sharing the difficult tale with him.

Over 50,000 names are etched in that black granite wall. Another million-plus Viet Nam vets carry scars or memories from the '60s and '70s that were their "personal problem."

No one supported or thanked those young heroes long ago. It's still not too late.

Steve